PEDRO CALDERÓN DE LA BARCA

Calderón was born in Madrid in 1600. On pain of disinheritance, his father demanded that he become a priest. His response was to abandon his studies and take up the 'dissolute' profession of poet and playwright – although he would enter the priesthood eventually in 1651. His first notable play, *Amor, honor y poder* (*Love, Honour and Power*) was performed in 1625, and he quickly established his reputations as both a formidable dramatist of the Spanish Golden Age, and a brawler, spending some years in exile. Admired for their poetic beauty and philosophical depth, Calderón's other plays include *La vida es sueño* (*Life is a Dream*, first published in 1635), *El Alcalde de Zalamea* (*The Mayor of Zalamea*), *La Dama duende* (*The Phantom Lady*), *La Devoción de la Cruz* (*Devotion to the Cross*) and *El Pintor de su deshonra* (*The Painter of Dishonour*). He was also a great favourite of the royal court, and was commissioned to write a number of elaborate spectacles by Philip IV. Calderón continued writing until the day of his death in 1681, even writing the very specific script for his own funeral.

HELEN EDMUNDSON

Helen Edmundson's first play, *Flying*, was presented at the National Theatre Studio in 1990. In 1992, she adapted Tolstoy's *Anna Karenina* for Shared Experience, for whom she also adapted *The Mill on the Floss* in 1994. Both won awards – the TMA and the Time Out Awards respectively – and both productions were twice revived and extensively toured. Shared Experience also staged the original adaptation of *War and Peace* at the National Theatre in 1996, and toured her adaptations of Mary Webb's *Gone to Earth* in 2004, Euripides' *Orestes* in 2006, and the new two-part version of *War and Peace* in 2008. Her original play *The Clearing* was first staged at The Bush Theatre in 1993, winning John Whiting and Time Out Awards, and *Mother Teresa is Dead* was premiered at the Royal Court Theatre in 2002. Her adaptation of Jamila Gavin's *Coram Boy* premiered at the National Theatre to critical acclaim in 2005, receiving a Time Out Award. It was subsequently revived in 2006, and produced on Broadway in 2007.

Pedro Calderón de la Barca

LIFE IS A DREAM

in a new version by Helen Edmundson

NICK HERN BOOKS

London

www.nickhernbooks.co.uk

A Nick Hern Book

This version of *Life is a Dream* first published in Great Britain in 2009 as a paperback original by Nick Hern Books Limited, 14 Larden Road, London W3 7ST

Reprinted 2011

This version of *Life is a Dream* copyright © 2009 Helen Edmundson

Helen Edmundson has asserted her right to be identified as the author of this version

Cover image: Dewynters
Cover design: Ned Hoste, 2H

Typeset by Nick Hern Books, London
Printed in the UK by CPI Antony Rowe, Chippenham, Wiltshire

A CIP catalogue record for this book is available from the British Library

ISBN 978 1 84842 060 1

Helen Edmundson's version of *Life is a Dream* was first
performed at the Donmar Warehouse, London, on 13 October
2009 (previews from 8 October), with the following cast:

ASTOLFO	Rupert Evans
ROSAURA	Kate Fleetwood
CLOTALDO	David Horovitch
CLARION	Lloyd Hutchinson
ESTRELLA	Sharon Small
SOLDIER 2 / SERVANT 2	David Smith
BASILIO	Malcolm Storry
SOLDIER 1 / SERVANT 1	Dylan Turner
SEGISMUNDO	Dominic West

Director	Jonathan Munby
Designer	Angela Davies
Lighting Designer	Neil Austin
Composer & Sound Designer	Dominic Haslam
Composer & Musician	Ansuman Biswas
Movement Director	Mike Ashcroft

Characters

ROSAURA
CLARION
SEGISMUNDO
CLOTALDO
ASTOLFO
ESTRELLA
BASILIO
SERVANT 1
SERVANT 2
SOLDIER 1
SOLDIER 2

Plus various soldiers, ladies-in-waiting, members of the King's court, servants and musicians

This text went to press before the end of rehearsals and so may differ slightly from the play as performed.

ACT ONE

Scene One

A steep mountainside. Poland. ROSAURA *enters. She is
dressed in a man's travelling clothes, and looks dishevelled.*

ROSAURA.
　　Horse! Where are you? Where are you? Horse!
　　Unnatural, deluded beast.
　　Do you think you are an eagle,
　　a hippogryph who dares to ride
　　and race upon a rampant wind?
　　You are lightning without its fire,
　　you are a bird without its plumes,
　　a fish without scales, a creation
　　most undeserving of your name.
　　Where are you? To which stark outcrop
　　of this confusing labyrinth
　　did you bolt, did you hurl yourself from?
　　Stay here then, and be the Phaeton
　　of the beasts. I myself, alone
　　and desperate, with only fate
　　to point the way, shall start down
　　this lofty mountain face, so cragged
　　and furrowed against the years of sun.
　　Oh, Poland. This is no welcome
　　for a stranger, demanding
　　that I register in blood
　　upon your soil. Hardly arrived
　　and such a hard arrival.
　　I cannot doubt what trials await me,
　　yet let there be some comfort
　　for my dismal and unhappy soul.

Enter CLARION, *a clown.*

CLARION.
> Your unhappy soul, then, is it?
> Just the one unhappy soul?
> I thought it was the two of us
> who started out on this adventure,
> two of us who, blow for blow,
> have battled all adversity,
> two of us who've tripped and rolled
> together down this mountainside.
> But no. I understand. I see.
> I'm wanted for the suffering
> but when it comes to the complaining
> it's all, 'Poor me, poor me, poor me.'

ROSAURA.
> Dear Clarion, I did not wish
> to claim your anguish for myself,
> and so deprive you of your share
> of consolation. For as the great
> philosopher says, there comes such ease,
> such satisfaction from complaint
> 'tis almost worth inviting pain
> in order to bemoan it later.

CLARION.
> I spit on your philosopher.
> He was a drunken old codger.
> I'd have dealt him a hefty slap
> and let him complain about that.
> But what do we do now, mistress?
> Look at us: horseless, afraid, lost
> in this empty wilderness,
> the sun's already on its way
> towards the next horizon.

ROSAURA.
> I never saw a thing so strange.
> If my eyes are not deceived
> by my imagination,
> in the eerie twilight of the day
> I think I can perceive a building.

CLARION.
>It may be wishful thinking,
>but I do believe I see it too.

ROSAURA.
>The merest glimpse of a simple
>tower, lodged so tight between
>the rocks, the light can barely reach it.
>So primitive is it, and set
>so low beneath the ambitious
>cliffs, it seems no more than a shaft
>of stone, fallen from the pinnacles
>and settled on the ground below.

CLARION.
>Let's go a little closer, shall we?
>No point in standing here and gawping.
>Let's go and ask whoever's home
>if they'll be kind and let us in.

ROSAURA.
>The door, like the mouth of a tomb,
>gapes open, and from its very depths,
>the encroaching night is born.

>*The sound of chains is heard.*

CLARION.
>Good God in Heaven, what's that I hear?

ROSAURA.
>My skin is ice. I burn with fear.

CLARION.
>The clanking of a chain. A soul
>from purgatory. I'd stake my life
>on it.

ROSAURA.
>It comes again.

Scene Two

SEGISMUNDO*'s voice is heard, off.*

SEGISMUNDO.
Oh, wretched me! Unhappy me!

ROSAURA.
Such sadness. I don't think my heart
can bear to face more torment.

CLARION.
I know mine can't.

ROSAURA.
                    Oh, Clarion.
I say the time has come to fly
these sombre and enchanted heights.

CLARION.
Oh, so do I. I'll fly with you.
I wish my legs were coming too.

ROSAURA.
But is that not a flickering light?
A single candle or a lamp,
which like some pale and tremulous star,
seems only to intensify
the closing darkness of the sky?
Yes. And by its rays I can discern,
the outline of a prison cell,
the coffin of a living corpse,
and more astonishing again,
beneath those pelts and skins of fur
there is a man weighed down by chains,
whose only comfort is that tiny light.
Clarion, how can we leave,
now we have seen his misery?

CLARION.
Well…

ROSAURA.
>Let us approach and listen.

>SEGISMUNDO *appears. He is bound with chains and dressed in animal pelts.*

SEGISMUNDO.
>Oh, wretched me! Unhappy me!
>Dear Lord in Heaven, tell me please,
>what harm does my existence mean
>that I should be so cruelly used
>as this? That I was born I do
>confess, and being born is Man's
>most heinous crime, deserving
>of severest judgement, yet and yet
>I cannot grasp nor comprehend
>what further crime I did commit
>that I should be condemned
>to such extremes of punishment.
>For are not all men born, as I?
>And given so, what mitigation,
>what rights are theirs which I, alas,
>am not entitled to employ?
>The bird is born and straightaway,
>leaving the confines of the nest,
>soars into the sky with boundless jòy,
>a flower of feathers, a dazzling
>bouquet in flight, it glides and sweeps
>unfettered to exultant heights.
>I have more soul than any bird
>and yet must I have less freedom?
>The beast is born, its patterned coat
>a miracle of nature's art,
>intricate as the distant stars,
>yet stirred by instincts hard and deep,
>it soon becomes a monster,
>a predator with claws and teeth
>that strikes with cold barbarity.
>I have more conscience than the beast,

and yet must I have less freedom?
The fish is born, sliding out from mud
and roe, a freakish thing that shuns
the very air. But once a vessel
on the seas, it dances through the water's
flow, voyages without a care,
the oceans' vast extremities.
I have more purpose than the fish,
and yet must I have less freedom?
The river's born, a silvery snake,
that curls and winds through hills and vales,
urging the budding land to wake,
the trees to blossom in its trail,
'til still at last upon the plain,
it melts into its own domain.
I have more life than any river,
and yet must I have less freedom?
I cannot contain the passion
which this stirs within my breast.
I am an Etna, a volcano,
I will choke upon my heart
and spew the fragments of my anguish
out into the air. Why? Why?
What law, cause, justice can deny
a man his liberty, a right
so pure, so vital it is granted
to the river, and to the fish,
to the beast, and to the bird?

ROSAURA.
His words have made me pity him
and yet I fear him too.

SEGISMUNDO.
                              Who's there?
Who's listening? Is it Clotaldo?

CLARION.
Say yes. Say anything.

ROSAURA.

It's I. (*Aside*.) God help me. (*To* SEGISMUNDO.)
    A piteous man,
who, wandering through these desolate caves,
could not help but overhear your sorrows.

SEGISMUNDO.

Alas, then I must kill you.
You cannot live and know my frailty.
You heard my words, and now I'm forced
to take you in these sinuous arms
and tear you limb from limb.

CLARION.

                                I'm deaf.

I didn't hear any of it.

ROSAURA.

I throw myself before your feet.
If you are human born, forgive me.

SEGISMUNDO.

Your voice alone would soften me,
your grace suffice to still my hand,
your gentleness to trouble me.
What magic is it you command?
I know so little of the world:
this tower has been my cradle
and my grave. And since my birth,
if you can call my advent so,
I have seen nothing but these wastes,
where I endure my sad existence,
an animated skeleton,
a body dead and yet alive.
I must astound you more, perhaps,
and make you think me monstrous,
for I have only ever seen
or spoken to one single man,
who listens to my endless woes
and tells me facts of Heaven and earth.

I am a prisoner, in truth,
shackled by these weighty chains
and trapped by my imaginings.
And though I've tried whene'er I can
to watch the creatures, birds and stars,
and estimate the ways of man,
I never thought, I never knew
there could be such a thing as you.
You calm me. My raging soul is still.
You charm my ears, enchant my eyes.
I have to look upon your face,
and with each look my wonder grows,
I have to look upon your face,
though I may die for gazing so.
For you are life, you are everything.
And life for a man who cannot
live is death. Then let me die.
It is as nothing, nothing
against the agony of pain,
the unendurable torture
it would be for me to turn
and take my eyes away from yours.

ROSAURA.

I don't know what to say to you.
I think the Heavens led me here
to bring me consolation,
though in a way I would not wish.
There is a fable tells a tale
about a man so poor, so low,
he lived upon the blades of grass
he gathered daily from the ground.
'Is there a soul on earth,' he asked,
'more poor and destitute than I?'
And then he learned the answer,
for standing still he turned around,
and there beheld another man,
picking up the scraps of grass
which he himself had thrown away.

I thought I was more piteous
and more ill-starred than anyone.
Yet if I were to look back now
I think you'd be behind me,
picking up my petty griefs and holding
them as joys. And if by any way,
by any means my sorrows
can alleviate your pain,
then listen to them, take them please,
for I would...

Scene Three

CLOTALDO *enters*.

CLOTALDO.

     Guards! Guards of the tower!
Do you sleep or are you cowards?
Intruders gain upon the prison!

ROSAURA.
What is this now? Who is this man?

SEGISMUNDO.
Clotaldo, my gaoler and my judge.
My woes have only just begun.

CLOTALDO.
Guards of the tower! Be quick! Look to!
Before they can defend themselves!
Capture them or kill them!

SOLDIERS.

     Seize them!

CLARION.
Guards of the tower! It's up to you,
but I'd say the capturing thing is easier.

CLOTALDO.
> Cover your faces, all of you!
> On no account must we be seen.

> *CLOTALDO enters, holding a shotgun. With him are several
> SOLDIERS, whose faces are covered by masks.*

CLARION.
> Oo, look, they're all in little masks!

CLOTALDO.
> You cannot know what you have done.
> This is a most forbidden place.
> No one, by order of the King's
> decree, can enter or lay eyes upon
> the monster who is kept within.
> Surrender to me. Drop your arms,
> or this gun, this metal snake,
> will shoot forth deadly poison
> with a force enough to shake the earth.

SEGISMUNDO.
> If you harm them, tyrannous Lord,
> I'll take my own life with these chains.
> I swear to God, though I am bound,
> I will rip myself to pieces,
> with my own hands, with my teeth, here,
> amongst these rocks, before I let
> you injure them.

CLOTALDO.
> Segismundo!
> You know full well you are so cursed,
> so misconceived, 'twas Heaven's will
> you died before you even lived.
> You are restrained to stop you acting
> on these abhorrent fits of rage.
> Then why do you make idle threats?
> (*To the* SOLDIERS.) Shut him inside! Hide him away!

The SOLDIERS shut him into his cell. From within:

SEGISMUNDO.

Oh, Heavens, you were wise and right
to keep me in captivity.
For I swear if I were free,
I'd rise up like a Titan now,
and, piling precious stone on stone,
I'd reach and smash the crystal sun!

CLOTALDO.

That's why you suffer as you do!

Scene Four

ROSAURA.

I see how much his pride offends,
and so I implore you humbly,
upon my knees, to spare my life.
Let my meekness touch your heart,
for 'tis a steely judge indeed
who does not heed humility.

CLARION.

And if neither pride nor meekness
have any power to soften you,
though don't forget they have won through
in countless other little plays,
then I stand poised between the two,
and urge you not to end our days.

CLOTALDO.

You there!

SOLDIER.

     Sir!

CLOTALDO.

        Take up their weapons.

Cover their eyes. They must not see
where they go or how they get there.

ROSAURA.
Wait, my Lord. This is my sword:
I give it up to you alone,
as right commander of these men.
It cannot be surrendered
to a person of inferior worth.

CLARION.
This is my sword: I'll give it up
to any old twerp. Here. Have it.

He hands his sword to the nearest SOLDIER.

ROSAURA.
And if I am to meet my death,
then I bequeath that sword to you.
I charge you, beg you, keep it safe,
for though I do not understand
the perfect secret it conceals,
I do know that its golden blade
is party to great mysteries.
Relying on its strength alone,
I came here to avenge my name
against a grievous wrong.

CLOTALDO (*aside*).
                              Great Heavens!
What is this I hear? My problems
and confusion, my fears and worries
start to grow. (*To* ROSAURA.) Who gave it to you?

ROSAURA.
A woman.

CLOTALDO.
                   What was her name?

ROSAURA.
I cannot tell you that.

CLOTALDO.

                    Why not?
Is it fanciful assumption
or can you say with certainty
this sword is master of some secret?

ROSAURA.

She who gave it to me said,
'Go to Poland, use your wits,
your skill and your determination
to ensure that lords and princes
see you with this priceless sword.
For one of them will then afford
you favour and protection.'
My saviour's name she would not speak
for fear that death had taken him.

CLOTALDO (*aside*).

Merciful God! What does this mean?
Is this real or an illusion?
I gave this very sword, I'm sure,
to the beautiful Violante.
It was to be a secret code,
a warning sign in years to come,
that whoever wore it round his waist
could claim from me a father's
love and all the warm devotion
that a man owes to a son.
But what do I do now? Oh, hideous
dilemma! For the person
wearing it has caused his death
by coming here, and kneels before me
with his life already forfeit.
How can this have come about?
Can fate be so perverse and fortune
so inconstant? This is my son.
The signs are echoed in my breast.
For my own heart leaps to look at him,
and like a lonely prisoner

who hears a once-beloved voice
beseech him from the street below,
it tests the shackles of my chest,
it presses hard against my eyes,
the windows of my soul, and seeps
through them as tears. What shall I do?
Oh, you Heavens, what shall I do?
If I now take him to the King,
well then, I take him to his death.
And yet I can't conceal his crime,
my duty to the King forbids it.
Love for what is truly mine
against my true allegiance.
I will be wrenched in two. But wait.
Does not my duty to the King
outweigh all life or private honour?
Then all is clear and duty wins.
And did this young man not proclaim
that he has come here seeking vengeance
for some grievance done to him?
A man who has been wronged has lost
his honour. Then he is not my son,
nor does he share my noble blood.
But what if it was not his fault?
What if his honour has been stained
in some way no one could prevent?
Honour is made of fragile stuff,
it takes but a breath to taint it.
Then what more could he seek to do?
What more seek to do than risk
his life by coming here to right
the damage done against him?
This is my son. He shares my blood.
His courage is the proof of it.
Caught between two paths of action.
I will take him to the King,
and tell the King most privately,
he is my son and he must die.
I hope this simple act of honour

will move my Liege to clemency.
And if I win my son his life
then I will help him to avenge
whatever wrong was done to him.
But if the King, unwavering,
should give him death, then he will die,
and never know I am his father.
(*To* ROSAURA *and* CLARION.) Strangers, you must come
    with me.
And do not think yourselves alone
in this, your great adversity.
I too am caught 'twixt life and death
and nothing could seem worse to me.

Scene Five

Music. Enter ASTOLFO, *with an escort of* SOLDIERS *on one side, and on the other side,* ESTRELLA *and her* LADIES.

ASTOLFO.
    The drums and trumpets, birds and streams
    do well to join their songs in praise
    of those exquisite orbs, your eyes,
    which burn like comets 'gainst the sky.
    Such is the power of your presence,
    such is the grandeur of your gaze,
    the trumpets seem to fly on feathers,
    the birds to sound a martial blaze.
    Their notes salute you as their queen.
    The birds salute you as Aurora,
    the trumpets as Minerva,
    the flowers as Flora. Rise then,
    Estrella, shame the day that parts,
    you are the light, the flower, the strength,
    the sovereign ruler of my heart.

ESTRELLA.

Words and actions should speak as one,
Prince Astolfo. You are quite wrong
to ply me with such gallantries
when all this force, this show of might,
which, be assured, I would not fear
to fight, lend to your words a hollow
ring. This eulogy does not reflect
your will. Remember it is base,
the lowest kind of treachery
to flatter what you mean to kill.

ASTOLFO.

You are mistaken, Estrella.
For I am all sincerity.
When Eustorgio the Third, King
of Poland, died, he left an heir,
Basilio and two daughters
who gave birth to you and I.
Of this, I know, you are aware,
yet let me speak the facts aloud
that we might be assured of them.
Clorilene, your worthy mother,
who now dwells in a better world,
was the first, the eldest daughter.
Fair and gracious Recisunda,
may the Heavens protect her,
was the second. She married
Muscovy and I was born.
Our uncle, King Basilio,
who is, alas, succumbing
to the scorn of time, as all men must,
was ever more devoted
to his studies than the fairer sex,
and was left widowed, without a child.
And so it is that you and I
aspire to Poland's throne. Your claim,
your mother was the eldest girl;
mine, that as a man 'tis right

and fit that I take precedence.
We both, of late, disclosed our wishes
to our uncle, who replied
we must at once be reconciled,
and he summoned us together,
at this place and at this time.
That's why I left dear Muscovy
and my beloved territories.
I did not come to conquer you,
but in the ardent hope, sweet coz,
that you would deign to conquer me.
May love, that most beneficent
of gods, have lent her wisdom
to the readers of the skies
who called this day auspicious.
Let us find a way to make you Queen,
but Queen with my complicity.
For your honour let my uncle
offer you his mighty crown.
But let it be my honest love
which grants to you his kingdom.

ESTRELLA.

My heart is somewhat moved, great Prince.
I'll match your generosity
and say, of course, that should I wish
this sacred Kingdom to be mine,
'twould be so I could make it yours.
Although I wonder if your love
is quite as honest as you claim.
The portrait hanging round your neck
would seem to tell a different tale.

ASTOLFO.

Why, that is easily explained.
And yet these drums deny us time.
The King and all his court arrive.

Scene Six

Trumpets and drums are heard. KING BASILIO *enters, with his* COURT.

ESTRELLA.
  Wise Thales,

ASTOLFO.
            Learned Euclides,

ESTRELLA.
  let me tenderly embrace you,

ASTOLFO.
  let me with a loving clasp,

ESTRELLA.
  as ivy winds about the tree,

ASTOLFO.
  lay my allegiance at your feet.

BASILIO.
  Niece, nephew, give me your hands.
  Since you are both devoted
  to my gentle governance
  and come to me with true affection,
  I give you my assurance,
  you will be pleased in equal measure.
  And as I share my heart with you,
  a heart which bears the weight of office,
  I only ask that you be silent:
  there will be much to wonder at.
  Most beloved niece and nephew,
  illustrious courtiers, subjects all,
  prepare to listen to me now.
  I am renowned throughout the globe,
  for my deep and tireless studies.
  And I have been immortalised
  in artist's paint and sculptor's stone

and called, 'The Great Basilio'.
You know it is the sciences
I value most and best of all,
purest mathematics, which I use
to steal away from time itself
the solemn right of prophecy,
and from experience the gift
to teach with every passing day.
For when I analyse my charts
they tell me what the future holds
for years, for centuries to come,
and all of time is nothing.
The clouds, those swirling mists of snow,
the sky, that shining arc of glass,
illuminated by the sun,
divided by the moon's bright path,
the planets, those diamond globes,
most radiant spheres, adorned by stars,
wherein the zodiac signs appear,
they are the study of my years.
They are my books, their luminous leaves
reveal a thousand symbols,
mapping out in strokes of gold,
events, both adverse and benign
which we are yet to see unfold.
All I have learned can't be explained.
And yet, what has befallen me,
that speaks in terms both clear and plain,
and so, I ask that you persist
in your attention. Please listen on,
for you will be amazed.
Some years ago, my loving wife
bore for me an ill-starred son,
for whose coming the Heavens
exhausted all their portents
before he passed into this life.
And so it was, night after night,
when he was lodged within her womb,

his mother, in her web of dreams,
had visions of a hideous beast,
a brute in human form, ripping
from inside her flesh, and as he dripped
and spat her blood, this savage,
monstrous man would murder her.
The day of her confinement came,
and true to all the prophecies –
for fate is never late and never lies –
he was delivered, at a juncture
in the skies when the almighty
sun, suffused with red, clashed violently
against the moon, and with the earth
a barrier between the two,
they fought, with their light and power
and strength, weapons more primal
than the sword. It was the most dread,
the most profound eclipse the sun
had known since it condemned
the death of Christ our Lord in blood.
The orb was so engulfed by flames
it seemed it would implode and fall.
The sky turned black, buildings shook,
clouds rained down a storm of rocks,
rivers rose and ran with gore.
And into this apocalypse,
my son, Segismundo, was born.
A fitting start for such as he.
He killed his mother with his birth
and so declared, 'Beware of me,
I will repay your love with scorn.'
I sought out answers in my charts.
I saw in them, and everywhere
that Segismundo was to prove
a desperate and a fearless man,
the harshest prince, a ruthless king.
He would divide his people's hearts,
and turn this land into a school

for murder, vice and treachery.
And driven by depravity
he would unleash his wrath on me,
force me to crawl upon my knees
and subjugate myself to him.
Alas, it pains my heart to say
that these revered and aged hairs
would have become a carpet
for his cruel feet to tread upon.
I could not doubt what I had seen.
My studies had ever served me well.
They were precise. Irrefutable.
I made a resolution:
I would discover whether knowledge
can outwit the stars themselves.
I told the world the child had died.
I had a tower built, up high,
hidden in the mountains, in a steep
and craggy place, cut off from the sun.
I called it a forbidden realm,
where none must stray on pain of death,
and now you know the reason why.
Prince Segismundo lives within,
a poor and wretched prisoner.
Clotaldo is the only man
ever to see or speak to him.
He has schooled him rigorously
in sciences and Catholic law,
and has been the only witness
to his unremitting misery.
It seems to me there are three things
which have to be considered here.
The first is that I, Poland, love
and care for you so much, I feel
it is my duty, my vocation,
to protect you from the tyranny
of a harsh, despotic king.
Then, I have to bear in mind

that if I take from my own blood
that basic right which solemn powers,
both human and divine, have chosen
to confer on him, 'tis not an act
of simple, Christian charity.
For who can say that I, myself,
in trying to stop a tyrant son,
am not a tyrant in his place,
committing sins of my own making?
Thirdly, lastly, we have to ask
if I was in the wrong to grant
such credence to the prophecies.
Perhaps the child was truly born
with tendencies to certain ways,
but tendencies can be constrained.
The most extreme and desperate fate,
the most intrinsic inclination,
the most relentless planet,
all can sway the human will
but they cannot dictate it.
Debating with myself, wavering
between these thoughts as I have done
for many years, I have, at last,
decided on a course of action
which will, I think, astonish you.
Tomorrow, I intend to place
Segismundo upon my throne.
He will be told he is my son,
destined, therefore, to be the King.
He'll sit beneath my canopy,
will rule and govern in my stead,
and you will pay obeisance.
My questions will be answered then.
If he is wise and calm and true,
confounding all predictions made,
then he shall stay, and one day reign.
And you will gain a natural prince,
who was in thrall to mountain gods,

trained amongst the birds and beasts.
But if he proves a wilful soul,
and master of a wicked heart,
then he will be at once deposed.
I'll throw him back into his gaol,
and know 'tis not barbarity
but just and fitting punishment.
And then, because I love you,
my loyal and gentle subjects,
you shall have heirs to grace the crown.
They will be my niece and nephew.
For their claims will be as one,
and united by their marriage vows
they will receive all they deserve.
This is what I order as a king,
what I ask for as a father,
what I argue as a scholar,
what I advise you as a sage.
And if, as Seneca once said,
a king is but a humble serf
of the republic, then this
is what I plead for as your slave.

ASTOLFO.

Please let me be the first to speak.
For as the man affected most
by this too strange and poignant tale,
in the name of all here present
I ask that Segismundo
be allowed to come forth now.
He is your son; it is enough.

ALL.

Bring forth our Prince! Let him be King!

BASILIO.

Subjects, I thank you for your loyalty.
Please know that it is highly prized.
But now, accompany my guests,

these Atlases, unto their rooms.
Tomorrow you will see my son.

ALL.

Long live great King Basilio!

All exit towards the palace. Before BASILIO *can leave,*
CLOTALDO, ROSAURA *and* CLARION *detain him.*

Scene Seven

CLOTALDO.

May I speak to you, my Lord?

BASILIO.

By all means. Tell me what you will.

CLOTALDO.

I do not have the heart to kiss
your royal hands, as is my custom.
For I have been confounded
by a sad and bitter blow.

BASILIO.

What's wrong?

CLOTALDO.

Disaster has befallen me.
A grave event which could have been
my best and greatest joy.

BASILIO.

Explain.

CLOTALDO.

This handsome, courteous young man,
through impudence or ignorance,
entered the forbidden tower.
He saw the Prince, my Lord, and now…

BASILIO.
> Enough. Enough, Clotaldo.
> If it were any other day,
> 'tis true this would have angered me.
> But the secret is revealed.
> It matters nothing that he knows.
> Attend me later if you will,
> for I have many things to say
> and many things to ask of you.
> Prepare yourself: for you must play
> a vital – nay, a leading role
> in the most inspired event
> this world has ever seen.
> And as you would not wish, I'm sure,
> these prisoners be made to pay
> for a careless oversight
> upon your soldiers' part, my order is
> that they be freed.

CLOTALDO.
> Thank you, my Liege.
> May you live a hundred centuries.

BASILIO *leaves*.

Scene Eight

CLOTALDO (*aside*).
> The Heavens have smiled upon me.
> I need not tell him he's my son
> now that I can pardon him.
> (*To* ROSAURA *and* CLARION.) Strangers, you have your
> liberty.

ROSAURA.
> I kiss your feet a thousand times.

CLARION.
I don't, but I'm very, very pleased.

ROSAURA.
You have given me my life, great Lord.
I will forever be your slave.

CLOTALDO.
It is not life I grant to you.
For when a noble man is wronged,
it is impossible he should live.
You came here seeking vengeance
for some great insult done to you,
therefore you came without a life.
Until a life has been avenged,
it cannot be a life at all.
(*Aside*.) We shall see his mettle now.

ROSAURA.
You're right. 'Tis true. I have no life.
But when I get my just revenge,
and I assure you that I will,
my honour shall be properly cleansed
of any stain. And so my life
will prove a precious gift indeed.

CLOTALDO.
Take back from me this burnished sword,
and never doubt its strength. Steep it
in your enemy's blood and claim
the vengeance which is yours. Any sword
that once belonged to me – I mean,
as this has done for the moments
that I've held it in my hand –
will guarantee your victory.

ROSAURA.
I buckle it around my waist
a second time and in your name.
As powerful as my enemy may be, I swear
I will prevail and win the justice due to me.

CLOTALDO.

How powerful is this man you seek?

ROSAURA.

I dare not say. I dare not speak
his name. Not because I question
the courage of your patronage,
more that I fear to lose your favour,
which has become so dear to me.

CLOTALDO.

You are more likely to retain
it, if you tell me who he is.
I'd rather be aware of him,
and careful not to help him.
(*Aside*.) I must know his identity.

ROSAURA.

I would not want you to believe
I scorn the trust you place in me,
so know, my Lord, that my opponent
is none other than Astolfo,
Prince and Duke of Muscovy.

CLOTALDO (*aside*).

Too much, too much for me to bear.
Now I know it's so much worse
than I had feared. I must hear more.
(*To* ROSAURA.) But were you not born in Muscovy?
Your Prince cannot have done you wrong.
Go back, then, to your country.
Forget the cause that brought you here.

ROSAURA.

He is my Prince, that much is true.
And yet I know he did me wrong.

CLOTALDO.

It is impossible, I say.
Even if he'd been so bold
as to lay hand upon your face.
(*Aside*.) God help me.

ROSAURA.

His offence was worse.

CLOTALDO.
Then tell me what he did. It cannot
be as bad as I'm imagining.

ROSAURA.
Very well. But given the respect
in which I hold you, the affection
which I have for you, I hesitate
to tell you that these clothes I wear,
my outward show is a sort of trick,
and not what it would seem. There.
I think you know. So if I'm not
what I appear, and Astolfo
came to make Estrella his own,
I think you know the kind of wrong
which he has done to me.
Forgive me. I can say no more.

ROSAURA and CLARION leave.

CLOTALDO.
Wait. Please! What labyrinth is this?
Reason itself is failing me
when it should be the silver thread
I count upon to lead the way.
She is a woman. And my child.
It is my honour bears the stain.
My enemy is more than great,
and I am but a lowly slave.
Oh, Heavens, I must trust in you
to guide me and to light me through
this treacherous, perplexing maze.
And yet, alas, I start to fear
there is no help can reach me here,
where earth and sky are dark and strange,
and all the world is unexplained.

End of Act One.

ACT TWO

Scene One

BASILIO *and* CLOTALDO *enter.*

CLOTALDO.
All is done and as you wished it.

BASILIO.
Tell me what happened, Clotaldo.

CLOTALDO.
I prepared the soothing potion
as you ordered. I mixed those herbs
whose extreme potency and scent
rob people of their speech,
render them strangers to themselves,
turn men into breathing corpses,
by putting them to such a sleep,
so deep, so overwhelming,
that all their strength and sense are gone.
You will need no convincing, Sir,
that such a spell is possible,
for how often have we seen
that nature is a treasure trove
for medicine to draw upon.
I took that drink, a careful blend
of henbane and of opium,
and went to Segismundo's narrow cell.
I sat and talked with him a while
of silent lessons he had learned
from mountains and the changing sky.
Then, to prepare him for the test,
to raise his thoughts, I drew his eyes
towards the mighty eagle,

who spurns the regions of the wind
to reach the higher spheres of flame,
becomes a soaring ray of light,
a comet, fierce and unrestrained.
I praised to him this lordly flight,
and said, 'However great that bird
may be, you have more rank, more worth
than he, and stand above them all.'
That was enough encouragement.
No sooner had I touched upon
the subject of nobility,
than he took on an air of pride,
and arrogant pomposity,
and, with his most eminent blood
awakened in his veins, he asked,
'Is there some natural law at work
within the kingdom of the birds
which makes one kind content to show
obedience to another?
At least I know that I'm enslaved
by force alone, by violence.
Never, of my own free will,
would I submit to anyone.'
So stirred was he by talk of this,
the very root of all his pain,
I saw no reason to delay;
I raised the goblet to his lips
and bade him drain the potion down.
The sweet elixir slid from cup
to throat, and as it reached his gut,
his strength to deepest sleep gave way.
A cold and clammy sweat appeared
upon his limbs and on his brow,
so fixed, so pale and stiff was he,
had I not known 'twas but a seeming
death, I would have thought him gone.
Then those men whom you entrusted
with the working of your plan,
arrived and took him to a carriage,

conveyed him to your private rooms,
which had been decked with excess splendour,
all pomp the palace can afford.
They settled him within your bed,
and, until the spell has faded,
they'll wait on him with all the care
with which they wait on you, my Lord.
Those were the orders which you gave.
If my good service in this task
has earned for me some small reward,
then all I ask, forgive me, Sir,
is that you tell me what you mean
by bringing Segismundo here
in such a strange and furtive way.

BASILIO.

I understand your doubts, my friend,
and you shall hear my reasoning.
Today he'll learn that he's my son,
a man of worth, a king-to-be;
should he find himself tomorrow,
as well he might, reduced again
to prison and to misery,
'tis certain that his sorry plight
would crush his spirits utterly.
Knowing his true identity,
what comfort could there be for him?
I want to leave an open door,
a chink of light, which will allow
us to profess that everything
he saw today was but a dream.
That way, I have the chance to make
my study of his inward nature,
and he the chance of consolation.
For if he wakes and finds himself
back in his cell, he'll think he dreamt
it all. And who could tell him 'no'?
For after all, my dear Clotaldo,
everyone who lives is dreaming.

CLOTALDO.

> I fear you are misguided, Sir,
> and I have many arguments
> to prove it. But too late now.
> It seems the sleeper is awake.
> Look there, he comes towards us.

BASILIO.

> It's time for me to slip away.
> You are his tutor. Go to him.
> He will, no doubt, be much confused,
> relieve his turmoil with the truth.

CLOTALDO.

> You sanction me to tell him all?

BASILIO.

> Yes. If he learns the way of things,
> and understands the prize at stake,
> he'll have more will to show us all
> that he is master of his fate.

> BASILIO *leaves*. CLOTALDO *prepares to speak to*
> SEGISMUNDO.

Scene Two

CLARION *enters and speaks to the audience*.

CLARION.

> Getting in here has cost me four
> terrific whacks with a halberd,
> from a soldier with an enormous
> beard, as red and rough as his temper.
> Beardy barbarian! Yes, you!
> Barbarous barbarian!
> I say get thee to a barber's!

Lose your beard, lose your temper!
Or keep your temper. Worth it, though,
for a front-row seat on what unfolds.
No ticket touts for me, oh no.
I'm broke, but I've got wit enough.
I'll get the best view through my cheek.

CLOTALDO.

Here's the servant of that lady,
that purveyor of miseries
who carried my shame to Poland.
Any news for me, Clarion?

CLARION.

I have this news for you, good Sir:
your kindness, which declared itself
the great avenger of the wrongs
done to my mistress, Rosaura,
has persuaded her to change
into her female clothes again.

CLOTALDO.

I'm glad. It was a risky ploy
and detrimental to her cause.

CLARION.

And this news: she has changed her name,
and now purports to be your niece,
and such great praise has come her way,
that she now lives within the palace,
lady-in-waiting to Estrella.

CLOTALDO.

It's only right that she should claim
the privilege due to her from me.

CLARION.

And this news: she awaits with hope
the glorious day when you step forth
to reinstate her honour.

CLOTALDO.
Tell her she does well to wait,
is right to put her faith in time.

CLARION.
And this news: she's highly favoured
and adored, feted like a very queen
because she's thought a niece of yours.
And this news: I, her faithful man,
though I'm connected to you too,
am left to fade away with hunger,
and no one spares a thought for me.
You all forget my name is Clarion,
and should this horn decide to call,
it could broadcast loud and clear,
a tale for everyone to hear,
about my mistress and Astolfo,
and about you too. Clarion –
secret. Secret – Clarion.
It's not a healthy mix at all.

CLOTALDO.
I understand your grievances.
I'll see that you have all you need.
Perhaps you should come and work for me.

CLARION.
Why, it would be my pleasure, Sir.
But look where Segismundo comes.

Scene Three

SEGISMUNDO *enters, with an entourage of* MUSICIANS *and* SINGERS, *and* SERVANTS *who are dressing him in fine clothes.*

SEGISMUNDO.
What am I seeing? What do I see?
Great God above, what does this mean?
I am amazed, yet feel no fear.
It's real, and yet how can it be?
Me, in sumptuous palace halls,
all draped with silks and tapestry,
with servants at my beck and call,
resplendent in shining livery.
Me, waking from the sweetest sleep,
in such a grand commodious bed,
with all these people dressing me.
I can't believe that I'm asleep,
my senses tell me otherwise.
But am I not Segismundo?
Heavens, explain this fantasy.
What can have happened while I slept,
what shift of my imagination
for me to find myself like this?
But then, what cause have I to care
for why or wherefore this came about?
I'll let myself be waited on,
and let things take the course they will.

SERVANT 2.
He seems disturbed and melancholy.

SERVANT 1.
I would be too, if I were he.

CLARION.
I wouldn't.

SERVANT 2.
>Speak to him. Go on.

SERVANT 1 *addresses* SEGISMUNDO.

SERVANT 1.
>Shall we tell them to sing again?

SEGISMUNDO.
>No. Bid them stop and leave me be.

CLOTALDO *approaches him*.

CLOTALDO.
>Your Highness. Great Lord. Allow me, please,
>to kiss your hand. Let my honour
>be the first to pay you tribute.

SEGISMUNDO.
>Clotaldo. You are Clotaldo.
>Why do you speak with such respect?
>In prison you abused me so.
>Tell me what's happening to me.

CLOTALDO.
>Your liberty, your altered state,
>are causing such profound confusion
>that your sense, your heart, your reason,
>are bound to be besieged by doubts.
>Allow me to dispel them all.
>Know this, my Lord. You are a prince,
>and heir to Poland's royal throne.
>If you were once removed from view,
>hidden, protected, shall we say,
>'twas but from fear of darkest fate,
>which augured for this blessed realm
>a thousand woes and tragedies,
>the moment that your head was crowned.
>But now, trusting you to overcome
>what the stars have long decreed,
>trusting you to take possession
>of yourself, your destiny,

you were brought, whilst lost in sleep,
from your tower unto this palace,
to claim at last your rightful place.
The King, your father, and my Lord,
will come to see you presently,
and you may learn all else from him.

SEGISMUNDO.

Oh, you vile and loathsome traitor!
'All else from him!' What else is there?
What else can matter to me now?
I know now who I really am!
Now all of you can start to learn
about my might, my pride, my power!
Traitor! Treacherous to your country,
treacherous to me. To lie to me.
To hide me from my proper self,
denying me against all reason
this, my rightful state.

CLOTALDO.

Oh, woe is me!

SEGISMUNDO.

You have betrayed the word of law,
you have pandered to the King,
maimed me with your cruelty,
and for these most appalling crimes,
the King, the law and I say death!
And at my hands.

SERVANT 2.

No, my Lord!

SEGISMUNDO.

Let no one try to stop me!
No one can, and as God lives,
if you get in my way, I'll throw
you from the casement there and watch
you break apart upon the ground!

SERVANT 1.
Run, Clotaldo!

CLOTALDO.
                    I pity you.
Such rampant pride, such gross conceit.
Don't you realise that you dream?

He goes.

SERVANT 2.
You ought to know…

SEGISMUNDO.
                    Get out of here.

SERVANT 2.
He could not but obey his king.

SEGISMUNDO.
Bad laws should never be obeyed,
though they be issued by a king.
I am his Prince.

SERVANT 2.
                    'Twas not his place
to question if 'twas good or bad.

SEGISMUNDO.
'Tis not your place to question me!

CLARION.
What the Prince says is very good.
You two, though, are very bad.

SERVANT 2.
Who gave you permission to speak?

CLARION.
That would be me.

SEGISMUNDO.
                    And who are you?

CLARION.
> I'm nobody and somebody.
> Sometimes I'm here. Sometimes I'm there.
> I'm the greatest fly-by-night
> this world has ever seen.

SEGISMUNDO.
> > You're funny.
> The first I've met in this new world
> who's been remotely nice at all.

CLARION.
> Oh, I'm undisputed champion
> at being nice to Segismundos.

Scene Four

ASTOLFO *enters*.

ASTOLFO.
> Oh, day of days! The light of Poland
> is awake, and our horizons
> blaze with joy and with a glow divine.
> You are a sun, arisen
> from the ground, a dawn that breaks
> from underneath the hills. Shine,
> shine forth, most-honoured Prince! Your head
> has long been due the laurel crown.
> May you wear it for eternity.

SEGISMUNDO.
> > God keep you too.

ASTOLFO.
> I must present myself, I think,
> so you may greet me with more honour.

Astolfo, born Duke of Muscovy.
Your cousin and your equal.

SEGISMUNDO.
Do I not show enough respect?
I have declared, 'God keep you.'
If that displeases you so much,
the next time we should chance to meet,
I'll tell God not to keep you.

SERVANT 2 (*to* ASTOLFO).
Great Prince, I beg you, bear in mind,
that he was raised in humble caves,
and treats all men accordingly.
(*To* SEGISMUNDO.) My Lord, Prince Astolfo must be
    shown...

SEGISMUNDO.
I did not like the high-flung way
in which he dared to speak to me.
Nor did he deign remove his hat.

SERVANT 2.
A privilege owned by such as he,
the most exalted members of the court.

SEGISMUNDO.
I am more exalted.

SERVANT 2.
              Etiquette
demands the very highest respect
exist between the two of you.

SEGISMUNDO.
Who gave you leave to lecture me?

Scene Five

ESTRELLA *enters*.

ESTRELLA.

Your Highness, welcome to the palace
and to the royal house of Poland.
It is with gratitude and pride
that we receive your presence here.
Let past deceits be set aside,
and may you reign immortal years,
august, beloved and revered.

SEGISMUNDO.

Beautiful, beautiful woman.
Who is this human goddess,
this deity suffused in grace,
this exquisite apparition?

CLARION.

That's your cousin, Sir. Estrella.

SEGISMUNDO.

Estrella, sovereign Lady,
your kind felicitations
for blessings lately come to me
are undeserved. For it is you,
the sight of you, which is the only
blessing I shall prize. Estrella.
'Twas wise to name you for a star.
Yet all the stars in all the Heavens
could not contain such perfect light.
Your radiance would shame the sun.
Give me your precious hand to kiss,
that tiny cup of virgin snow,
from which the air drinks purest white.

He takes her hand and kisses it, but does not stop there.

ESTRELLA.

You are a trifle bold, my Lord.

ASTOLFO (*aside*).
    But what is this? That's not her hand...

SERVANT 2.
    This cannot pass. I'll intervene.
    Your Highness, you are too forward.
    Especially so, since Prince Astolfo...

SEGISMUNDO.
    I told you not to question me.

SERVANT 2.
    I'm only saying what is right.

SEGISMUNDO.
    Do you seek to anger me?
    What I want, is what is right.

SERVANT 2.
    You wish me to obey and serve.
    You would not have me shirk my duty.

SEGISMUNDO.
    Did you not heed my warning?
    Oppose me once again, my friend,
    and I will hurl you to your death.

SERVANT 2.
    You would not dare to treat me so.

SEGISMUNDO.
    No? Well, by God, I mean to try!

He picks up the SERVANT *and exits towards the window.*

ASTOLFO.
    Is he in earnest? Stop him now!

All rush after SEGISMUNDO.

ESTRELLA.
    Help here! Someone stop him! Please!

After a moment, all but ESTRELLA *return.*

SEGISMUNDO.
He tumbled from the balcony.
He may be lucky. There was sea below.
But still. God lives. I managed it.

ASTOLFO.
Learn to control your temper, Sir.
As a palace to a wilderness,
so is a man unto a beast.

SEGISMUNDO.
Speak like that to me again,
and you may find you have no head
to keep that hat of yours upon.

ASTOLFO *leaves*.

Scene Six

BASILIO *enters*.

BASILIO.
What has been happening here?

SEGISMUNDO.
                              Nothing.
There was a man who kept annoying me,
so I threw him off the balcony.
He wouldn't fit through the window.

CLARION (*to* SEGISMUNDO).
This fellow is the King, my Lord.

BASILIO.
Say you have not killed a man,
the very day of your arrival.

SEGISMUNDO.
He dared me, and I won the wager.

BASILIO.

    I'm very sorry, Segismundo.
    I had come to find you here,
    knowing that you'd been appraised
    of your position, expecting
    to find you rising up triumphant
    above your destiny and stars.
    And lo, your first act is murder.
    These arms of mine were primed with love,
    yet how can they embrace you now?
    Who can gaze without repugnance
    at a dagger used to kill?
    Who can see blood upon the ground,
    where another man was slain,
    without a sense of deepest horror?
    It is a natural response,
    e'en for the hardiest of men.
    And so I, looking at your arms,
    see but an instrument of death,
    and will not come towards you.
    I will forgo your arms' embrace.
    Your arms are frightening to me now.

SEGISMUNDO.

    I'll live without your false embraces,
    as I have always had to do.
    A father who has treated me
    with merciless severity,
    who has raised me as a creature,
    caged me like a monstrous beast,
    and wished and hoped that I would die –
    what care I for such a father's love?
    It has pleased you to deprive me
    of everything that makes me human.

BASILIO.

    Would that I had stuck to my resolve!
    Would that I had spared the Heavens
    the lash of your audacity!

SEGISMUNDO.

Why give me life and then proceed
to take that life away from me?
To give is the finest act of all.
To give then take away again
is low and base in the extreme.

BASILIO.

Is this your way of thanking me?
When you have found yourself transformed
from lowly prisoner to Prince?

SEGISMUNDO.

Why should I give you thanks for that?
Tyrant! Despot! You are old
and past your prime. If you die now,
with what would you endow me?
With nothing more than what is mine.
You are my father and you are King,
so all this wealth, this power, this prize
is what is due to me by right.
I say it's you who should account
for all the missing years of light,
the theft of my honour and my life!
Give thanks that I don't make you pay.
'Tis you who is in debt to me.

BASILIO.

You insolent savage!
What the Heavens foretold is true,
and 'tis to them I now appeal
against you and your dangerous pride.
So you've discovered who you are,
and think yourself above us all,
but you had better heed these words:
show more humility, more care.
Though you may know that you're awake,
beware, you might be dreaming.

BASILIO *leaves, followed by his* COURT. *Only* CLARION
remains close by.

SEGISMUNDO.
'Though I may know that I'm awake…'
This is no dream. I can feel things.
I believe in what I was,
and I believe in this. Old man,
you may regret what you have done,
but it's too late to change it now.
Rage, then. Grieve. Bewail your fate.
For I was born to wear this crown,
and you cannot be rid of me.
I know exactly who I am:
a deadly cross 'twixt beast and man.

Scene Seven

ROSAURA *enters, dressed now as a woman.*

ROSAURA (*aside*).
I had to come here with Estrella,
but I am dreadfully afraid
that I might chance upon Astolfo.
Clotaldo said he mustn't see me,
or guess my true identity,
and I am in Clotaldo's hands,
and mean to trust his good advice.

CLARION.
Of all the wonders that you've seen
today, what's been your favourite thing?

SEGISMUNDO.
Little has astonished me,
for I was schooled and well prepared.
One thing alone has touched my soul,
taken my senses unaware:
the loveliness of womankind.
In one book I was made to read,

it said that God spent all his time
creating man, a world in miniature.
But I say, if that's really so,
'tis woman who amazes me,
for in her beauty and her grace,
He's tamed and captured Heaven.
A woman's beauty is to man's
as distant as Heaven from the earth.

He has seen ROSAURA.

Further, if the woman be her –

ROSAURA (*aside*).
    That must be the Prince. I must go.

SEGISMUNDO.
    Wait, Lady. Don't take the light away
    by fleeing at my first approach.
    Allow me the semblance of a day.
    But what is this? What do I see?

ROSAURA (*aside*).
    Impossible. And yet it's true.

SEGISMUNDO (*aside*).
    I've seen this beauty once before.

ROSAURA.
    I've seen this strength, this majesty,
    degraded by a prison's walls.

SEGISMUNDO.
    I have found my life. Woman,
    for that is compliment indeed,
    the greatest one a man can pay,
    who are you? You must tell me, please.
    I felt at once that I adored you,
    even before I saw your face.
    A sort of faith compelled my words.
    I know I've seen those eyes before.
    But where? And how? Who are you, Lady?

ROSAURA (*aside*).
  I mustn't tell him who I am.
  (*To* SEGISMUNDO.) I am a servant to Estrella.

SEGISMUNDO.
  No. Say rather that you are the sun,
  by whose bright flames that star survives,
  enhanced by your reflected rays.
  The rose is sovereign of the flowers
  because her scent surpasses all.
  The diamond reigns amongst the gems,
  unequalled in her brilliance.
  Venus is empress of the stars,
  worshipped for her peerless light.
  Whilst in the planets' restless court,
  all praise the sun's transcendent might.
  So if, in realms of earth and Heaven,
  'tis always beauty which excels,
  how is it that you come to serve
  one who is far less beautiful?

Scene Eight

CLOTALDO *enters, unseen by* SEGISMUNDO *and* ROSAURA.

CLOTALDO.
  'Twas I who brought this monster forth,
  it falls to me to bring him down.
  But, no. What's this? What's happening here?

ROSAURA.
  Your praise and favour honour me.
  Your words have left me reeling, Sir,
  and silence must speak my reply.

  She starts to go.

SEGISMUNDO.
>No, please don't go, I beg of you.
>You can't condemn me to the dark.

ROSAURA.
>Yet I must go, with your permission.

SEGISMUNDO.
>And what if I won't give permission?

ROSAURA.
>Well, then, I fear that I must take it.

SEGISMUNDO.
>Then gallantry will fall away.
>I cannot tolerate resistance,
>it is as poison to my patience.

ROSAURA.
>I did not mean to anger you.
>And from respect, I'll keep my patience,
>even if you abandon yours.

SEGISMUNDO.
>My trembling awe of your perfection,
>will not, I fear, prevail for long.
>I like to have what I can't have,
>I like to do what I can't do.
>It's a challenge, a test, you see.
>I threw a man from that balcony
>today, because he said I couldn't.
>So it's entirely possible,
>that just to discover if I can,
>I'll throw away your honour too.

CLOTALDO.
>He threatens her. Oh, you Heavens!
>What am I supposed to do?
>My honour is at risk again,
>the target of a mad desire.

ROSAURA.

It's true, then, what they say of you:
that you are shameless, base and cruel,
and should you ever rule this land,
'twould be a wild and godless place.
Prove them right. Why shouldn't you?
You are a man by name alone,
a savage, a brute, an animal.

SEGISMUNDO.

Insults, my Lady? Such wounding words,
when I have shown you courtesy,
and thought to get it in return.
But I am cruel, and when I'm done,
you'll know that more than anyone.
(*To* CLARION.) Leave us! See the door is shut and
    barred!

CLARION *leaves*.

ROSAURA.

I'm lost. Listen…

SEGISMUNDO.

                    I'm a tyrant,
a beast. Nothing can appease me now.

CLOTALDO.

He's too strong. I have to stop him.
Even if he kills me for it.
Segismundo! Wait! Listen to me!

SEGISMUNDO.

What, you? You dare to rile me twice?
You ancient fool! You pointless relic!
Are you not mindful of my wrath?
How do you come to be in here?

CLOTALDO.

I heard your voice, and came to say,
tread carefully if you wish to reign.
No amount of tyranny

will guarantee the power you seek
if this should prove to be a dream.

SEGISMUNDO.

Why this talk of dreams again?
I'll cut your tiresome throat for you,
then we shall see who dreams!

ROSAURA.

Oh no!

SEGISMUNDO *goes to draw his sword*. CLOTALDO
kneels in front of him, and tries to stop him.

SEGISMUNDO.

Get your insolent hand off me!

CLOTALDO.

Help here! I'll not let go. Help here!

ROSAURA.

Oh, Lord in Heaven!

SEGISMUNDO.

Let go I say,
you toothless cur, or with these arms
I'll crush your feeble life from you!

They fight.

ROSAURA.

Someone! Quick! He's killing Clotaldo!

Just as CLOTALDO *falls at* SEGISMUNDO*'s feet,*
ASTOLFO *enters and stands between them*. ROSAURA
rushes off before he sees her.

Scene Nine

ASTOLFO.

But what is this, my noble Prince?
You would not soil your shining sword
with such inept and weary blood?
I pray you, return it to the hilt.

SEGISMUNDO.

Not until the slaughter's done,
and it's been christened in his gore.

ASTOLFO.

My feet are now his sanctuary.
I can't withdraw and watch him die.

SEGISMUNDO.

Then you will die instead of him.
And let your death be my revenge
for all injustice done to me.

ASTOLFO.

'Tis no offence against the crown
if I defend my life.

They draw their swords.

Scene Ten

BASILIO *and* ESTRELLA *enter.*

CLOTALDO.
Be careful! Don't provoke him, Sir.

BASILIO.
Swords, here?

ESTRELLA.
                    Oh no. It is Astolfo!

BASILIO.
Explain this outrage. What's happening?

They sheath their swords.

ASTOLFO.
Nothing, my Liege, now you are here.

SEGISMUNDO.
Plenty, my Liege, though you be here.
I tried to kill that cringing traitor.

BASILIO.
Do you not see his silver hairs?
They alone should warrant your respect.

CLOTALDO.
He cares not a jot, for them or I.

SEGISMUNDO.
You really think a few grey hairs
will guarantee respect from me?
I live to see your ashen skull
contrite and trembling at my feet,
braced against the mortal blow
of my deserved and just revenge.

SEGISMUNDO *leaves.*

BASILIO.
No, no, my Prince, before you do,
you'll be asleep and in your tower,
and all that's passed today will seem,
like everything we most desire,
the distant promise of a dream.

BASILIO *and* CLOTALDO *leave*.

Scene Eleven

ASTOLFO.
Ill omens never lie, it seems.
They are blackly accurate.
'Twould be a great astrologer
indeed who only read disasters,
for all his portents would come true.
Good omens are a different thing
and rarely prove decisive.
Take Segismundo and myself:
cruelty, conceit, miseries, murders,
those were the predictions made for him,
and they were right on every count.
But I, Estrella, I looked upon
your eyes, those glorious rays of light,
forgot the sun, which seemed a shadow
in comparison, and saw a sky
alive with possibility and joy.
And it was right and it was wrong.
For even as I start to bask
in the brightness of your favour,
I feel the chill of your disdain.

ESTRELLA.
I doubt not the veracity
of the compliments you pay me,

but save them for another lady,
whose portrait hung around your neck
when you first arrived. She alone
is worth such costly flattery.
Ask her to pay you in return.
Compliments and vows of faith,
forged to obtain a different love,
are not good currency with me.

Scene Twelve

ROSAURA *enters, unseen by* ASTOLFO.

ROSAURA.
Here is a sight to end all sights.
At least my torments are complete,
for nothing could be worse than this.

ASTOLFO.
That portrait shall be banished
from my breast, and in its place
I'll set an image of your radiance.
For where Estrella rises,
there can be no shadows cast.
I'll go and fetch it instantly.
(*Aside.*) Forgive me this offence, Rosaura.
But men and women left alone,
have ever been unfaithful.

He leaves.

ROSAURA.
Oh, were I close enough to hear
his words. But he must never see me.

ESTRELLA.
Astrea!

ROSAURA.

      Oh! Yes, my Lady?

ESTRELLA.

How glad I am of your devotion.
I have a secret I must tell,
but would confide to you alone.

ROSAURA.

I am your humble servant, Ma'am.

ESTRELLA.

Though you have not been with me long,
still you have won my trust and love.
I dare to share my heart with you,
disclose those things I often hide,
even from myself.

ROSAURA.

      You honour me.

ESTRELLA.

Astolfo is to marry me.
'Tis hoped this single act of faith,
will wipe out countless miseries.
This much you know, Astrea.
But here's the thing: the day we met
it shocked and grieved my heart to see
the portrait of another woman,
fixed on a chain around his neck.
I asked him about it, quietly,
and being the gentleman he is,
he swore he would relinquish it.
He's gone to find it, even now.
I fear 'twould be embarrassing
for him to put it in my hand.
Stay here for me, and when he comes,
take the portrait in my stead.
I need say nothing more, I'm sure.
You're young and beautiful yourself,
and understand the ways of love.

ESTRELLA *leaves*.

ROSAURA.
　　Would that she had kept her secret!
　　Oh, Heavens, is there woman born
　　with wit and wisdom half the match
　　for such a situation?
　　Was ever anyone but I
　　besieged by such misfortunes,
　　beset by such battalions
　　of grief? What am I to do?
　　Clotaldo, whom I owe my life,
　　my liberty and sanctuary,
　　instructs me to conceal my name,
　　to hide my true identity,
　　and I would not incur his wrath.
　　But if I see Astolfo now,
　　what subterfuge can I employ?
　　My words, my voice, my eyes can try
　　to hide the truth from him, and yet
　　my soul will contradict their lies.
　　What shall I do? Why should I care?
　　No matter how much I prepare,
　　agonise, deliberate,
　　when the dreadful moment comes,
　　I'll be in thrall to my despair.
　　No one gets the better of their pain.
　　And since there is no help for it,
　　I'll let my pain encompass all,
　　surrender to my wretchedness
　　and end all doubts and all pretence.
　　Until that time, be with me, Lord.

Scene Thirteen

ASTOLFO *enters, with the portrait.*

ASTOLFO.
Here is the portrait, my Lady.
But, my God!

ROSAURA.
                    What's wrong, Your Highness?
What makes you so astonished?

ASTOLFO.
You ask me that? When it is you
I look upon, Rosaura,
when it's your voice that speaks to me.

ROSAURA.
Rosaura? Forgive me, Your Highness,
but I fear that you mistake me
for another. I am Astrea,
a humble servant most unworth
such great surprise and consternation.

ASTOLFO.
Stop this pretense, Rosaura.
Enough. The soul can never lie.
Though you may greet me as Astrea,
my love receives you as Rosaura.

ROSAURA.
I don't know what you mean, my Liege,
and so am lost for my reply.
All I can say is that Estrella,
the brightest of all Venus' stars,
asked me to await you here,
to collect for her that portrait.
She told me why she wanted it,
and bade me take it straight to her.
They were Estrella's commands.

And though such very simple things
seem strangely hard for me to do,
we must obey Estrella's will.

ASTOLFO.
That's very good, Rosaura. Yes.
But no matter how you try,
you won't succeed in fooling me.
Your eyes should listen to your voice.
Each of your well-tuned instruments
must be compelled to play off-key,
if you want this false ensemble
to drown the music of your heart.

ROSAURA.
I'm simply waiting for the portrait.

ASTOLFO.
Very well. Since you must persist
with this deception, I'll join in.
Astrea, kindly tell your mistress
I hold her in such high esteem,
that when she asks me for a portrait,
I do not feel it is enough
for me to simply proffer one.
And so I'm sending the original,
for her to cherish and revere.
Then take it to her, would you, please?
It is in your possession,
as much as you possess yourself.

ROSAURA.
When a person dares risk all
to find and claim a certain thing,
he's bound to feel dejected, small,
if he goes back without it.
I came here for that portrait, Sir,
and even though I may possess
a work of art with greater worth,
I will not leave until it's mine.

ASTOLFO.
>But what if I will not oblige?
>How do you think to get it then?

ROSAURA.
>Like this. (*She tries to snatch it*.) Let go, you selfish wretch!

ASTOLFO.
>It's no use. You'll never get it.

ROSAURA.
>As God lives, this will not fall
>into another woman's hands!

ASTOLFO.
>Control yourself. Have you no shame?

ROSAURA.
>I am beyond shame. You traitor!

ASTOLFO.
>Be calm now, my Rosaura.

ROSAURA.
>Don't call me yours. You liar, you villain!

Scene Fourteen

ESTRELLA *approaches*.

ESTRELLA.
>Is something wrong? Astrea?

ASTOLFO.
>It's Estrella. Be quiet now, please.

ROSAURA (*aside*).
>Love, grant me ingenuity.
>I have to get my portrait back.
>(*To* ESTRELLA.) My Lady, allow me to explain
>what's happening here.

ASTOLFO.
                            What game is this?

ROSAURA.
  I waited here, as you commanded,
  to collect the portrait you desire.
  Finding myself alone a while,
  my mind began to flit about
  from one thing to another,
  and your mention of a portrait
  reminded me that in my pocket,
  I keep a portrait of myself.
  I drew it out to look at it,
  simply to pass the time away,
  and accidentally dropped it.
  The Prince, who had just then arrived,
  with that other lady's likeness,
  saw it and seized it instantly.
  It seems he is so loath to part
  with the portrait you requested,
  he thought to give a different one.
  I pleaded with him desperately,
  begged him to return my picture,
  but he refused. At which, I grew
  quite angry and impatient
  and tried to snatch it back from him.
  The one he's holding now is mine.
  Please look, you'll see that it's my face.

ESTRELLA.
  Astolfo, give me the portrait.

  He does so.

ASTOLFO.
  My Lady…

ESTRELLA.
                  It's very good.
  Exceptionally true to life.

ROSAURA.
It's mine, you see?

ESTRELLA.
                    Beyond a doubt.

ROSAURA.
Now ask him for the other one.

ESTRELLA.
No. Take your portrait and leave, Astrea.

ROSAURA (*aside*).
I've got it back. That's all that matters.

She leaves.

Scene Fifteen

ESTRELLA.
Hand me the other portrait, please.
I don't suppose I'll ever see,
or ever speak to you again,
but given that I, foolishly,
requested that you give it up,
I cannot let you keep it now.

ASTOLFO (*aside*).
How do I get out of this one?
(*To* ESTRELLA.) Most exquisite and divine Estrella,
much as I would love to serve
and to obey your every wish,
I cannot give you what you ask…

ESTRELLA.
Oh, you vile and faithless lover!
Wretched man! Damn your portrait!
Why should I desire it now?

A humiliating keepsake
of a time I cared to rule your heart.

ESTRELLA *leaves*.

ASTOLFO.
Wait, Estrella. Listen to me.
My God, Rosaura, when, how, why,
did you follow me to Poland?
You rush us both to our perdition.

Scene Sixteen

SEGISMUNDO *is revealed as he was at the start of the play, in animal skins. He is sleeping. Two* SERVANTS *and* CLARION, *place him back on the floor of his cell.* CLOTALDO *looks on.*

CLOTALDO.
Leave him there. This is where it started,
and now this is where it ends.

SERVANT 1.
I'll put the chains back as they were.

CLARION.
Don't wake up, Segismundo, friend.
You'll only find yourself bereft,
your fortunes all reversed again,
your glory nothing but a sham,
your life a shadow and your death
the only hope of light. Sleep well.

CLOTALDO.
How very deep and philosophical.
I think you need some time alone
to complete your meditations.
(*To the* SERVANTS.) Seize him. Lock him in the other cell.

CLARION.

What do you mean? Not me? Why me?

CLOTALDO.

Because the Clarion knows too much,
and prison is the only way
to stop him calling to the world.

CLARION.

But this is mad! For pity's sake!
Is it me who wants to kill
my father? Did I throw that squawking
Icarus off the balcony?
Was it me who died and then awoke?
Am I sleeping? Am I dreaming? No.
Then why do you imprison me?

CLOTALDO.

Because your name is Clarion.

CLARION.

I'll change it then. I'll be a flute,
they're very soft and secretive.
I'll be a bell, a steeple bell,
and only ring to pass the time.
I swear to you.

CLOTALDO.

Secure him well.

CLARION *is taken away.*

Scene Seventeen

BASILIO *enters, his face covered*.

BASILIO.
Clotaldo.

CLOTALDO.
Your Majesty!
But why do you risk coming here?

BASILIO.
Fool that I am, I had to see
what's happening to Segismundo.
Oh, what grief this is to me.

CLOTALDO.
There he is. Back in his pathetic
state of old.

BASILIO.
Unfortunate Prince.
Why were you born at such a time?
Wake him now. We need not fear:
the lotus water which he drank
has stripped him of all strength and power.

CLOTALDO.
He's restless, my Lord. He's talking.

BASILIO.
I wonder what he dreams. Let's listen.

SEGISMUNDO (*as he dreams*).
For it's a good and godly prince
who puts an end to tyranny.
Clotaldo must die at my hands.
My father must crawl at my feet.

CLOTALDO.
He threatens me with death again.

BASILIO.
And me with shameful degradation.

SEGISMUNDO.
Let this peerless, valiant man,
enter the theatre of the world,
step out upon its mighty stage
that I might wreak my vengeance.
Let them see Prince Segismundo...
(*He awakens*.) But where am I?

BASILIO.
                      I can't be seen.
You know what to do, Clotaldo.
I'll be listening from over there.

   BASILIO *retreats to a corner.*

SEGISMUNDO.
Am I myself again? How come?
Am I the me that once I was?
A prisoner weighed down by chains,
condemned for all eternity?
Tower, are you not my tomb? Yes.
Yes. My God. What things I've dreamed.

CLOTALDO.
Ah. It's time to wake up, I see.

SEGISMUNDO.
Yes. It is time to wake up.

CLOTALDO.
You should not waste the day in sleep.
Have you not awoken once,
since we marvelled at the eagle's
flight, and I left you here alone?

SEGISMUNDO.
No. Nor have I awoken now.
Clotaldo, I think I'm still asleep.
And why should I assume I'm wrong?
For if it's true that I imagined

all those things that went before,
that seemed so real, so palpable,
then I must question everything.
I know I'm tired, but what of that?
When I'm asleep I see reality,
when I'm awake, why, then I dream.

CLOTALDO.
Tell me about the things you dreamed.

SEGISMUNDO.
I can't tell you what I dreamed, Clotaldo,
but I will tell you what I saw.
I woke up and I found myself
(oh, sweet torture) in a bed,
so soft, and of such gentle hues,
it might have been a nest of flowers,
woven by the spring itself.
A multitude of noble lords,
kneeling in homage at my feet,
hailed me as their one true Prince,
offered me garlands, jewels and robes.
Then you appeared and raised my heart
unto a sphere of highest joy:
you told me I was Prince of Poland.

CLOTALDO.
For which, I hope, I was rewarded.

SEGISMUNDO.
You were not. For with an iron fist,
and heart as bold and fierce as fire,
I denounced you as a traitor,
and twice I tried to murder you.

CLOTALDO.
Were you so harsh to me, young man?

SEGISMUNDO.
Yes. I was incensed by all,
and sought revenge on everyone.

There was one woman whom I loved.
That part was true, if naught else was.
For all the rest is over now,
and yet my love, my love remains.

BASILIO *is overwhelmed and slips away.*

CLOTALDO (*aside*).
His Majesty is moved to tears,
and cannot bear to listen more.
(*To* SEGISMUNDO.) I think I see the cause of this:
we talked of Man's inherent might,
then straightaway you fell asleep,
and so your dreams became whole empires.
But though you dreamt, I must confess,
I wish you'd used with more respect,
the man who's taught and cared for you,
despite all risk, your whole life through.
Even in sleep, Segismundo,
a little goodness never goes amiss.

CLOTALDO *leaves.*

SEGISMUNDO.
There is some truth in what he says.
If I should ever dream again
I must contain my rage and wrath,
and stifle rank ambition.
For I will dream, as will we all,
because this life, this world of ours
is so mysterious, so strange,
it seems to me, to live at all
is just the same as dreaming.
I think I understand that now.
We dream our lives until we wake.
A king is dreaming he's a king,
and all the tributes he receives,
are not, in truth, possessed by him,
for they exist upon the wind,
and in the end will turn to dust.

And who would ever choose to reign,
knowing they would one day wake
into the deeper sleep of death?
The rich man dreams the precious wealth
which gives him so much cause to worry.
The poor man dreams the hardship
and the burden of his poverty.
The man who's starting out in life,
the man who labours, hopes and schemes,
the man who errs and acts from spite,
all are dreaming, each one dreams,
yet none of them perceives it quite.
I dream I am a powerful prince:
I dream I cower within these walls.
And both are true, and both are lies.
What is this life? A trick? A story?
An episode of passion?
A shadow, a delirium?
A vast imperfect fantasy,
where even the greatest good of all,
is nothing but futility?
Why do we live? What does it mean?
When dreams are life, and life's a dream.

End of Act Two.

ACT THREE

Scene One

CLARION *is languishing in his prison cell.*

CLARION.
  I know nothing. I know nothing.
  Still here. Imprisoned in this magic
  tower. Left to rot for what I know.
  There's a lot more that I don't know.
  Can't they let me out for that? Eh?
  It's terrible. A tragedy,
  to do this to a man like me,
  a man with special needs like mine.
  I can't stand quiet. It's in my name:
  Clarion. I can't stand silence.
  The only things to talk to here
  are spiders and rats and little
  birds who sometimes stop to say hello.
  Poor me. Who wouldn't pity me?
  Last night I had disturbing dreams.
  My sorry head's still full of them.
  They started well: trumpets everywhere,
  horns, processions, drums, laughter,
  then crosses, whips and flagellants,
  some crawling uphill, others down,
  and all around them, men and women
  fainting to look upon the blood.
  I'm fainting now from lack of food.
  For trapped in my religious cell,
  I'm forced to sit here day on day,
  studying the philosopher
  Nothingtoeat, and the dictats
  of the Council of Nosupper.

Silence is holy, so they say,
so when the new year comes around,
I'll claim Saint Secret as my patron,
and I shall fast upon his day.
Such punishment will be deserved,
for he who plays a servant's part
yet still contrives to hold his tongue,
is the most blasphemous of all.

Scene Two

Drums and crowds are heard. Voices from within:

SOLDIER 1.
>This is the tower where he is kept.
>Down with the door! Forward, everyone!

CLARION.
>Christ alive! They're looking for me!
>They must be, for I heard them say
>I'm here. What do they want with me?

>SOLDIERS *enter.*

SOLDIER 1.
>Inside. Search the place.

SOLDIER 2.
>   Here he is!

CLARION.
>Oh, no he isn't.

ALL.
>   Your Majesty...

CLARION.
>I think they're drunk.

SOLDIER 2.
                              You are our Prince.
And we will never be content
with any but our rightful lord.
Accept our love.

ALL.
                              Long live our Prince!

CLARION.
This all seems real enough to me.
Perhaps it's the custom in this place,
to make a new man prince each day,
then lock him back into the tower.
I must assume my character.

ALL.
Give us the royal feet to kiss.

CLARION.
One's feet are needed for oneself.
A wobbly prince is no use to anyone.

ALL.
We told your father, with one voice,
that our allegiance lies with you,
and not the Prince of Muscovy.

CLARION.
You dared to speak so to your King?
Then I declare you are a bunch of very naughty men.

SOLDIER 1.
'Twas loyalty, Sir, sincerely meant.

CLARION.
In that case, I shall pardon you.

SOLDIER 2.
Leave this prison and liberate
your empire! Long live Segismundo!

ALL.
Hurrah!

CLARION.
>Did they say Segismundo?
Ah, well. Perhaps that's just the name
they give to all imprisoned princes.

Scene Three

SEGISMUNDO *enters, having been released by other*
SOLDIERS.

SEGISMUNDO.
Who speaks the name of Segismundo?

CLARION.
Oh. I'm understudy after all.

SOLDIER 2.
Which is Segismundo?

SEGISMUNDO.
>I am.

SOLDIER 2.
So why said you, you stupid fool,
that you were Prince Segismundo?

CLARION.
I never mentioned Segismundo.
'Twas you who Segismundoed me.
So stupid fool yourself.

SOLDIER 1.
>Great Prince,
these colours and these arms are yours.
For it's our strong and fervent prayer,
you will consent to be our Lord.
Your father, King Basilio,
fearful of the prophecy,
but minutes since, recalled his court,

and means to hand your power and rights
to Astolfo, Duke of Muscovy.
The people, Sir, the rank and file,
knowing now that you exist,
will not accept a foreign prince,
nor hold him as their sovereign.
And so, my Lord, with bold disdain
for that dark fate the stars foretold,
we've come here to this prison cell,
and do beseech you, take control,
command these men, quit this tower,
lay claim upon your crown and sceptre,
wrench them from the tyrant's hands.
Come. Beyond these staunch, imposing walls,
there stands an army, mightier still,
a force of rebels and citizens,
who shake this desert with your name.
Liberty awaits you. Hear them,
Prince –

VOICES.

     Long live Segismundo!

SEGISMUNDO.

Again? Heavens, must you torture me?
Would'st have me dream once more of power,
for time to make me small again?
Would'st have me chasing glory
in the twilight and the shadows,
only for a waking wind
to show me all was vanity?
The things you speak of cannot be.
What shall I believe in next?
That all the world exists in peace?
That men have found humility,
and live in truth and harmony?
I know this life is but a dream.
And you are the departed ones,
phantoms who trick my deadened mind

with your pretence of flesh and blood.
I do not trust your feigned obeisance,
nor my fictitious majesty.
They are illusions, visions all,
that will dissolve by light of day,
like blossoms that mistake the spring,
and wither in the frost of dawn.
No more, I say. I know you now,
and I'll no longer be deceived.

SOLDIER 2.

But, good my Lord, I swear it's true.
Look out upon those mountain heights.
See all the people gathered there,
awaiting you and your commands.

SEGISMUNDO.

I saw such wondrous sights before,
as clearly as I see this now,
and they all proved to be a dream.

SOLDIER 2.

But dreams are sometimes premonitions
of great events about to pass.
So with your dream, Your Majesty.

SEGISMUNDO (*aside*).

A premonition. Why, there's a thought.
Then I should heed the lesson taught.
And since this life is too soon done,
let's dream again, my soul, let's dream.
But this time I'll be on my guard,
and poised to snap myself awake,
whene'er the moment's right for me.
Deceit is nothing, once perceived.
And if forewarned, a man can make
a mockery of the direst fate.
And now I truly understand
that power is a fleeting thing,
which always will and always must

be borrowed from the Maker's hand;
then I say, we are armed, my friend,
and need not shrink from anything.
(*To* ALL.) Subjects, I thank you for your faith.
You have your Lord. You have your Prince.
Follow me. Be loyal to me,
and with Godspeed I'll set you free
from foreign rule and slavery.
To arms! For soon you'll see my worth.
I'll join in battle with the King.
I'll bring the Heavens' prophecy
crashing down upon this earth.
I'll see the tyrant on his knees!

ALL.
Long live Segismundo! Hurrah!

SEGISMUNDO (*aside*).
Unless I choose to wake up first.

Scene Four

CLOTALDO *enters*.

CLOTALDO.
What in God's name is happening here?

SEGISMUNDO.
Clotaldo.

CLOTALDO.
No! Segismundo!
(*Aside*.) What horrors will befall me now?

CLARION.
I hope he chucks him off a cliff.

CLARION *leaves*.

CLOTALDO.

I fall before your feet, my Lord,
and reconcile myself to death.

SEGISMUNDO.

Get up, old man. Be my pole star,
be my guide. The one I trust
to keep me on a righteous path.
All that I am, I owe to you,
to your due care and loyalty.
Give me your arms.

CLOTALDO.

Can this be true?

SEGISMUNDO.

I'm dreaming, and would do some good.
For goodness never goes amiss,
even in the land of sleep.

CLOTALDO.

If that is so, Your Majesty,
and goodness is the watchword here,
then I must speak for your own good,
and risk our newfound amity.
If you mean war against your father,
then I implore you, think again.
I could not counsel or condone
the slightest force against my King,
nor would I help you in your cause.
'Tis said now. Kill me if you will.

SEGISMUNDO.

Ungrateful villain! Traitor!
But no. I must restrain myself.
I still don't know if I'm awake.
I envy you your bravery,
Clotaldo, and thank you for it.
Go then. Go and serve Basilio.
I'll see you on the battlefield.
The rest of you, sound the call to arms.

CLOTALDO.

Words cannot speak my gratitude.

SEGISMUNDO.

With fortune for my comrade now,
this Prince will soon become a King.
If I'm asleep, don't let me wake.
If this is real, don't let me dream.
However this has come to pass,
I'll follow virtue to the last.
For if it's true, then good is all,
if false, let goodness break my fall.

All exit as the call to arms is sounded.

Scene Five

At the palace. BASILIO *and* ASTOLFO *enter.*

BASILIO.

Astolfo, Astolfo. Better to bid me throw
myself beneath the hooves of a stampeding horse,
bid me dam the mighty river's course that rushes
in torrents to the sea, or hold the basalt rock
in place when it would tumble from the mountain peak.
All easy, easy feats compared with making halt
the wild and reckless rampage of the common mob.
They are divided, split into opposing factions,
the chilling echo of their cry reverberates
around the streams and valleys at the mountains' feet.
Some cry, 'Astolfo!' and others, 'Segismundo!'
The throne is but an afterthought, a secondary
prize for them, beyond the expulsion of their rage.
Yet soon it will become the stage for that grim drama,
where fortune must play out her bloody tragedy.

ASTOLFO.

>Sire, let all the joy, the plaudits and acclaim
>that once you promised would be mine, be set aside.
>If Poland, where I hope to reign, resists me now,
>then I must act to earn and merit her respect.
>Give to me a valiant horse and set me on its back.
>I'll come down like a thunderclap upon the fray.

He leaves.

BASILIO.

>And hasten the inevitable. For that is all
>we serve to do. There's no defence 'gainst what's foreseen,
>and to attempt to change what's written, is but to cry out,
>'It will come!' Oh, cruel unyielding fate. Dread destiny!
>Why did I begin this? In seeking to protect
>this land, I've damned myself and all my people.

Scene Six

ESTRELLA *enters.*

ESTRELLA.

>Your Highness. Great King. The tumult is spreading
>everywhere, erupting in every street and square,
>swelling in one group, then the next. You must step forth.
>Use your weight and majesty to stop this madness,
>or you will see your kingdom drowning in a crimson
>tide, choked by the living scarlet of its own blood.
>There is naught but sadness now. All is carnage.
>All disaster. Your empire is on the brink of ruin.
>So ghastly is the bloody mood that grips the streets,
>that eyes see only horror, ears hear only grief.
>The sun has dimmed. The wind blows in upon itself.
>The stones are all for burial mounds, the flowers for wreaths.
>Each house is but a tomb, each soldier wears the face
>of death.

Scene Seven

CLOTALDO *enters*.

CLOTALDO.

>Thank God! Thank God I reach your feet alive!

BASILIO.

My Lord, the people, that blind and mindless monster,
breached the tower walls and drew your son from out its
>depths,
who, finding for a second time his status raised
to Prince and heir, displayed great bravery and strength
and swore to bring the prophecy crashing down
upon the earth.

BASILIO.

>Bring me a horse! I too have strength,
and I will use it now to finish my ungrateful
son. I ride out to defend my crown. 'Twas I who caused
this dreadful plight, now let my sword set all to rights.

He leaves.

ESTRELLA.

And I shall ride beside him. And like Minerva
shall I fly on outstretched wings. I'll set my name
forevermore, beside that goddess, born for war.

She leaves, and the call to arms is sounded.

Scene Eight

ROSAURA *enters and stops* CLOTALDO.

ROSAURA.
 I know the valour in your breast
 is crying out to be unleashed,
 but I must beg a word before
 I lose you to the battlefield.
 My Lord, Prince Astolfo saw me.
 Though I endeavoured earnestly,
 to follow all your wise commands,
 yet still I could not hide from him.
 And now I truly understand
 the depths of his contempt for me,
 for though he knew me instantly,
 he still would have Estrella's hand.
 Tonight he'll meet her in the garden.
 There is a gate. I have a key.
 I'll let you in, and trust in you
 to free me from my misery.
 For you are great and bold and true,
 and you will champion my honour,
 and do what you resolved to do:
 avenge me by Astolfo's death.

CLOTALDO.
 The moment I encountered you,
 your tear-filled eyes were not deceived,
 I felt entirely bound to do
 everything you could ask of me.
 And since that time, I've never ceased
 to plot your honour's safe return,
 and have imagined, I concede,
 killing the Duke of Muscovy.
 What a mad and desperate thought!
 Though honour would allow it,
 for the man is not my King.

It came to be my main intent,
until the day that Segismundo
held my life beneath his sword,
and he, the goodly Prince Astolfo,
rushed at once to my defence,
ignored the danger he was in,
and showed respect and care for me
beyond the call of chivalry.
Then how am I to take the life
of someone to whom my very soul
gives thanks for having rescued mine?
Torn between gratitude and pride.
'Twas I who granted you your life,
and he who gave my life to me.
So, tell me, how should I proceed?
I'm bound to you by what I gave,
to him, by what I did receive.
I, who ever lived to act,
can see no course of action now,
to comfort my divided heart.

ROSAURA.

I'm sure I need not tell you, Sir,
that for all men of highest birth,
it is as noble to bestow,
as it's ignoble to receive.
Adhering to that principle,
you have no cause to give him thanks,
for he bestowed your life on you,
and forced you to a shameful deed.
It was offence he offered you.
And yet to me, you are in debt:
for I enabled you to give,
and so enriched your great esteem.
You gave me, what you got from him.
And that is why you have to try
to salvage my imperilled honour:
as giving is above receiving,
so must I be above the Prince.

CLOTALDO.

It's true: there is nobility
in giving. But in receiving
there is gratitude. I am known
to be a man of honour.
And, because I choose to give,
people call me generous too.
Then let them also call me grateful:
for in all men of highest birth,
charity and gratitude
are qualities of equal worth.

ROSAURA.

Yet I remember when you said
a person wronged could have no life.
If that is so, well then, my Lord,
you've given me nothing after all.
To prove your generosity,
you must reclaim my life for me.
Giving is the greatest gesture:
be generous first and grateful later.

CLOTALDO.

I bow to your philosophy.
Your argument has won me round.
I will be generous, Rosaura.
I will bequeath you all my land,
and you must to a convent flee.
This kingdom is upon its knees,
ravaged by war and anarchy,
I'll not deliver grief on grief.
This solution settles all:
you fly the damage done to you,
take refuge in a cloistered life,
whilst I show loyalty to my King,
show generosity to you,
and to Astolfo, gratitude.
It is as much as I can do.
And as God lives, I'd do no more,
even if I were your father.

ROSAURA.

> My father? Ha! If you were so,
> I might submit to this dishonour,
> but you are not and so I won't.

CLOTALDO.

> Then, tell me what you mean to do.

ROSAURA.

> To kill the Duke of Muscovy.

CLOTALDO.

> You would not dare. A girl like you,
> uncertain even of your birth.
> You think that you could see it through?

ROSAURA.

> Yes.

CLOTALDO.

> Aided by who?

ROSAURA.

> By my good name!

CLOTALDO.

> Listen to me: In Astolfo…

ROSAURA.

> Who has cast my honour away…

CLOTALDO.

> You see, at once, your king-to-be,
> and fair Estrella's husband.

ROSAURA.

> No!
> He'll never live to see that day.

CLOTALDO.

> This is madness.

ROSAURA.

> I say so too.

CLOTALDO.
Then conquer it.

ROSAURA.
                    That I can't do.

CLOTALDO.
Then you will lose…

ROSAURA.
                    I know. I know.

CLOTALDO.
Your life and honour.

ROSAURA.
                    So be it!

CLOTALDO.
Then what?

ROSAURA.
                    I die.

CLOTALDO.
                    You'd die from spite?

ROSAURA.
From honour.

CLOTALDO.
                    From folly.

ROSAURA.
                    From courage.

CLOTALDO.
From passion.

ROSAURA.
From anger. From rage!

CLOTALDO.
                    Is there no cure for this obsession?
Is there nothing to be done?

ROSAURA.

>Nothing.

CLOTALDO.
Can't you search for other ways?

ROSAURA.
To Hell? This is my only path.

ROSAURA leaves.

CLOTALDO (*aside*).
My daughter. If you must damn yourself,
then wait, and let's be damned together.

Scene Nine

The countryside. Enter SOLDIERS, *marching. Enter*
SEGISMUNDO *and* CLARION, *both dressed in animal skins.*

SEGISMUNDO.
If Rome in its ascendancy
could only look upon me now,
how stunned, how staggered it would be
to witness this beguiling sight:
an animal striding at the head
of a great and fearless army,
the power of whose united breath
could blow the stars from out the skies!
But spirit mine, stay close to me,
I mustn't let this seeming glory
seduce me into vanity.
For if I wake and find it gone,
'twould weigh upon me heavily.
The less I win, the less I miss,
when all dissolves and vanishes.

A trumpet sounds.

CLARION.

>But see – upon that speedy horse,
>the sight of which, as it draws near,
>moves my rough heart to poetry
>(bear with me, it's not my idea),
>upon that horse, which seems to me,
>a map of all the world itself,
>its body being solid earth,
>its foaming mouth, the raging sea,
>the wind, the panting of its breath,
>whilst in the furnace of its chest
>there burns all Hell's ferocity,
>and part on part, whose hectic form
>evokes a chaos that dazzles me,
>upon that horse, monster of fire,
>of land and sea, dappled in colour,
>sleek of mane, swept on by spurs
>to such a pace it seems to fly,
>upon that horse (who wrote this verse?),
>a marvellous woman now arrives.

SEGISMUNDO.

>Her splendour overwhelms my eyes.

CLARION.

>Saints alive! I'd say that's Rosaura.

SEGISMUNDO.

>The gods have brought her back to me.
>Withdraw. I'll speak to her alone.

>CLARION *withdraws*.

Scene Ten

ROSAURA *enters, wearing a riding skirt, and a sword and dagger.*

ROSAURA.
Oh, generous Segismundo,
whose most heroic majesty
is now emerging from the night
of its obscurity into
the day of its great deeds;
I ask that you extend your care
to a sad and desperate soul,
who throws herself before your feet.
For she is woman, and misused,
two reasons which, e'en separately,
would be enough to move a man
of courage to defend her rights.
Three times now have you looked on me
in wonder, and three times failed
to recognise my face. For each
of those times I've come to you
in different clothes and different form.
'Twas as a man I met you first,
in that bleak prison where your woes
made mine seem easier to bear.
The second time, I was a girl,
a maid who caught and held your gaze,
when all your finery and power
were but a dream, a masquerade.
And so the third time is today:
I come to you, a freakish breed,
neither one thing nor another,
adorned as woman, armed as man,
and beg you, hear my tragedy.
I was born in the court of Muscovy,
to a fine and noble mother,
who, victim of her beauteous face,

attracted grave misfortune.
A feckless man laid eyes on her,
a man whose name I cannot give,
for it remains unknown to me,
though of his rank I have no doubt,
knowing my own worth as I do.
I am the flesh of his idea.
My mother, though rarest of her sex,
owned yet a woman's tender heart,
was swayed by charm and flattery.
He swore that he would marry her,
that reckless young philanderer.
So moved, so overwhelmed was she,
it vindicates her even now.
And when he left, which soon he did,
as Aeneas to his Carthage Queen,
he gave to her his golden sword.
It's hidden in my scabbard here,
and I'll unsheathe it by and by,
when my account is out and done.
From that loose knot, which does not bind,
be it a marriage or a crime,
some would say both, some would say none,
I was born, the very likeness
of my dam, if not in looks
then in my deeds and my mistakes.
Her fate was mine. I'll not say more,
except to name the man who stole
the jewels of my good name and honour,
robbed me of my self-respect:
Astolfo. To name him fills
my heart with rage, as though I name
a bitter enemy. Astolfo
is that indecent lord who spurned
this prize he had secured,
left me to rot, for when love's gone,
all courtesies are soon forgot,
and came to seek Estrella's hand.

Wronged and scorned, incensed, distraught,
a hell took hold within my heart.
I swore I would not speak again,
and built for me a silent wall.
Until one day, when all alone
with my mother, Violante,
she breached the line of my defence,
and out they poured, my torments
and my griefs. I felt no shame,
for she knew feelings all as mine,
had tried my food for poison.
She met each word with kind compassion,
and in her wish to ease my cares,
recounted sorrows of her own.
And learning lessons from her past,
she told me not to trust in time,
but bade me follow my seducer,
and force him with prodigious deeds
to grant my honour back to me.
She dressed me then in male attire,
that further harm be kept at bay,
and from the wall took down this sword.
See how distinctly it's engraved,
so too her words upon my heart –
'Go to Poland, use your wits,
your skill and your determination,
to ensure that lords and princes
see you with this priceless sword.
For one of them will then afford
you favour and protection.'
And so I came. And though Clotaldo
readily embraced my plight,
he has just now abandoned me,
and urges me to stand aside
and let Astolfo wed his queen.
Oh, brave and strong and mighty Lord,
whose day of vengeance has arrived,
I see you rise to Heaven's command,

and take up arms against the man
who served you with such cruelty.
Your wounds are keen and deep as mine.
I come to join you in your cause,
Diana in my rich attire,
Minerva in my armour.
Neither of us wants to see
Astolfo married to Estrella,
I, because he's bound to me,
you, because their coupled force
would jeopardise your victory.
As a woman I am here
to beg you to restore my honour,
and as a man I beg you too,
to take the crown that should be yours.
As a woman have I come
that gentle words might earn your pity,
as a man I kiss your sword
and swear to you my fealty.
As woman I must ask your help,
as man I bring my help to you.
And if, as happened once before,
you think this woman ripe to woo,
then as a man I'll use my sword.
For on this line I'm forced to walk,
I must be meek and mighty too.

SEGISMUNDO (*aside*).
Heavens, if I'm really dreaming,
let me dismiss this strange diversion.
My concentration and my strength
are filled past their capacity
without this tale of abject woe.
It is no care of mine. And yet,
if all I saw before was dreamt,
how come this woman saw it too,
and can recall such facts to me?
Then it was true. And so is this.
Confusion on confusion grows.

Is it that a true success
is so akin to what we dream,
that we cannot believe in it,
and fly to our imagined joys?
Or is the craft of our mind's eye
so skilful in its artistry,
the fake becomes the thing itself?
All and nothing then is real.
If that is so, then we should glean
from this opaque and shifting time,
whatever pleasure's there to take.
She's at my mercy, in my thrall,
this ravishing creature I adore,
so let's enjoy this moment.
Let passion break all virtue's laws,
and lust betray her suppliance.
I'll dream me my fulfillment.
But what of Heaven? Ay, what indeed?
Is any fleeting, earthly joy,
worth the loss of that divine
and everlasting glory?
Desire is but a dancing flame,
extinguished by the merest breeze.
Then let us mind eternity,
where love dies not, nor pleasures sleep.
Rosaura has no honour now.
'Twould be a right and princely deed
to win her honour back for her.
Then, as God lives, it must be done,
e'en before I claim my throne.
But oh, what sweet temptation.
Monster, turn, and walk away.
(*To* ALL.) Give the signal to attack.
This battle must be fought today,
before the Heavens' golden rays
are drowned in murky waves of night.

He prepares to leave.

ROSAURA.

My Lord, wouldst leave me in this way?
Are all my cares and my confessions
not worth a single word from you?
What, am I invisible?
Can you not see me, hear my voice?
Will you not even look at me?

SEGISMUNDO.

Rosaura, for your honour's sake,
'tis necessary to hurt you now,
that I might prove your saviour.
My voice declines to answer you
because my valour surely will,
I do not need to speak to you
for in my deeds you'll hear my words,
and if I cannot look at you,
'tis only that my self-restraint
cannot defeat your beauty.
I'll look me to your honour's fate,
and serve you with my duty.

He leaves.

ROSAURA.

But what exactly does he mean?
After all that I've endured,
must I be left to wonder still?

Scene Eleven

CLARION *enters*.

CLARION.
Are you receiving visitors?

ROSAURA.
Oh, Clarion! Where have you been?

CLARION.
Locked away inside a tower,
gambling to save my skin.
Would I lose, or would I win?
I came up trumps and now I'm free.
The best card, though, is up my sleeve.

ROSAURA.
What card?

CLARION.
Let's just say I know
the truth of how you came to be.
It seems Clotaldo… But what's that?

Drums are heard.

ROSAURA.
It comes this way.

CLARION.
A mighty force
is marching though the palace gates,
and falls on Segismundo's men!

ROSAURA.
Then I shall fight beside him.
This is no time for girls or cowards,
I'll prove the truth of my renown.

She leaves.

Scene Twelve

VOICES.
Long live our undefeated King!

OTHER VOICES.
Long live the fight for liberty!

CLARION.
Long live them both! And long live me.
That's the most important thing.
And, oh no, look, in all this haste
I find that I've been left behind.
Then I shall take on Nero's part,
when all was lost he paid no heed.
And if I feel the urge to fiddle,
I'll have to fiddle with myself.
(*He hides*.) This is my spot, my sanctuary.
Tucked away between these rocks,
I've got the whole show in my sights.
Death, you'll never capture me.
So here's to you – and now, goodnight.

Scene Thirteen

Fighting is heard. Enter BASILIO, CLOTALDO *and*
ASTOLFO, *fleeing*.

BASILIO.
Lives a more wretched king than I?
A father more dishonoured?

CLOTALDO.
The palace is lost. Your army
runs, retreats in fear and disarray.

ASTOLFO.

The traitors have their victory.

BASILIO.

But no, in conflicts such as these,
loyalty lies with those that win,
and those that lose are traitors.
Clotaldo, it seems we have no choice:
let's fly the callous vengeance
of a brutal and malignant son.

Shots are heard. CLARION *staggers, wounded, from his
hiding place.*

BASILIO.

My God!

ASTOLFO.

Who is this piteous soldier,
all wet and stained by his own blood?

CLARION.

I am a sad, unhappy man,
a man who tried to hide from death,
who, in running from its clutches,
hurtled straight into its arms.
There is no hole, no nook on earth
where death cannot discover you.
And so, turn back, rejoin the fray,
you're safer 'midst the swords and guns
than in a mountain hideaway.
No path is safe from fate's dark hand:
You'll die when death and God command.

He dies.

BASILIO.

'You'll die when death and God command.'
How well he voices our mistake,
our foolishness, this sorry corpse,
who preaches through his wound's bright mouth
and teaches with a bloody tongue.

In vain, in vain, do men resist
the workings of a higher power.
I only wished to save my realm
from all the horrors prophesied,
instead I find I've hastened her
into the pit of her demise.

CLOTALDO.

Fate may well know all the paths,
the corners where we seek to hide,
but it's not Christian to say
there is no place beyond its reach.
There is, my Lord. A man who's wise
can triumph over destiny.
Though you have suffered untold pain,
you can achieve salvation.

ASTOLFO.

My Liege, Clotaldo counsels you
with all the wisdom of his age.
I, though, am inflamed by youth,
and I would urge a different course:
in a dense and leafy thicket,
concealed upon this mountainside,
there is a horse, as swift as wind –
take her, and I'll guard your flight.

BASILIO.

If God intends that I should die,
if death awaits me in this place,
I shall not hide, but seek it out,
and rush to my allotted fate.

Scene Fourteen

A call to arms is sounded. SEGISMUNDO *enters with all his* FOLLOWERS, *including* ROSAURA. ESTRELLA *enters on* BASILIO*'s side.*

SOLDIER 1.
Behind the bushes or the trees,
somewhere on this mountainside
is where the King is hiding now.

He begins to search.

SEGISMUNDO.
Follow his lead! Spread out and search!
Miss not a single slope or branch.

CLOTALDO (*to* BASILIO).
Run, my Lord!

BASILIO.

I shall not flee.

ASTOLFO.
But why?

BASILIO.

Stand aside, Astolfo.

CLOTALDO.
But what do you intend to do?

BASILIO.
Something, my friend, I have not tried.
Prince Segismundo, here I am!
Your prey is found and at your feet.
Wipe then your boots upon this head,
trample this neck and crush this crown.
Besmirch the gift of my respect,
and spit upon my decency,
take your revenge upon my name,
a prisoner must you make of me.

And when all stands as was foretold,
pay tribute then to destiny
and let the Heavens' will be done.

SEGISMUNDO.
Illustrious court of Poland,
witness to so many wonders,
I bid you, listen to your Prince,
for he has much to say to you.
What the Heavens have determined,
what God has etched, e'en with a finger,
upon the blue slate of the sky,
whose symbols are the golden letters,
which glisten in the firmament,
these things cannot deceive or lie.
The liar, rather, is the man
who seeks to penetrate their secrets,
that he might make ill use of them.
My father, this man before you here,
seeking to escape the ruin
of what had been foretold of me,
made me a brute, a human beast.
And whereas the dreadful knowledge
of what I could, or might become,
combined with my nobility,
coupled with my gracious blood,
could have made me more humane,
more kind and mild than anyone,
the treatment which he chose for me
made me a wild and desperate thing.
'Tis all so obvious to see.
If a man is told, 'Beware,
one day a beast will eat your heart,'
should he then search out wolves and bears
and wake them from their slumbers?
If he is told, 'You'll meet your death
by that same sword around your waist,'
would he then draw, and to his chest
press hard the metal of its blade?

If he is told, 'Great walls of water
will sweep you to a silvery grave,'
should he at once set out to sea,
to scale the summits of the waves?
That's how my father dealt with me.
And even if my murderous nature
were like that quiet and sleeping bear,
my violence, that sheathed and waiting sword,
my silence, the calm before the storm,
you cannot hope to conquer fate
with cruelty and vengeful hate.
That only makes it more extreme.
Instead, proceed with moderation,
with care, respect, humility.
Then, after all has come to pass,
the humble soul may be reprieved.
Let these sad and strange events,
this horror, this grief, this spectacle,
serve as a lesson to us all.
After all his best attempts
to change the course of what was meant,
here is a father in my thrall,
a monarch crushed and swept aside.
This was the Heavens' judgement.
He could not win. So then, could I?
Who am inferior to his years,
his courage and his wisdom?
Stand up, my Lord. Give me your hand.
Now that the Heavens have prevailed,
and your remorse is clear to see,
I beg you, take your just revenge,
and I surrender at your feet.

BASILIO.
Such nobility. Such grace.
My son, my child, you are reborn
deep in the chambers of my heart.
You are a prince – our Prince by rights,
the laurel and the palm are yours.

Your victories are manifold,
your deeds more priceless than the crown.

ALL.

Long live Prince Segismundo!

SEGISMUNDO.

This day has been a day for valour.
One battle more requires my strength,
the greatest battle of them all,
for winning, I defeat myself:
Prince Astolfo, give your hand
unto the beauteous Rosaura.
In honour it is owed to her.
For honour I will see this done.

ASTOLFO.

I must confess… I own it's true:
I am beholden to this woman
for promises I made to her,
and yet, the question of her birth
is one that cannot be forgot.
'Twould be as poison to my pride,
a lapse, a slur upon my name,
were I to take her as my wife…

CLOTALDO.

Astolfo, wait, and speak no more.
Rosaura is a match for you
in her nobility and worth.
And with this sword I'll disabuse
whoever thinks to doubt my word.
I guard her with a father's love.

ASTOLFO.

What do you mean?

ROSAURA.

                    What did you say?

CLOTALDO.

I felt I must conceal the truth

until her honour was restored.
The story is too long to tell.
In brief, she is my daughter.

ROSAURA.

Then I'm complete.

ASTOLFO.

This changes all.
I'll gladly join my heart with yours.

SEGISMUNDO.

Estrella, look not so dismayed.
We see that you have lost a prince
of courage and outstanding fame,
then let me make you some amends,
and ask that you become my Queen.
I cannot claim a history
as proud or fortunate as his,
and yet I am his equal.
Lady, I offer you my hand.

ESTRELLA.

I'll take this happiness you grant,
and am assured of so much more.

SEGISMUNDO.

Good Clotaldo, you have served
my father with great loyalty:
my arms are ever there for you,
and all your wishes shall be mine.

SOLDIER 1.

If that's how you reward a man
who wasn't even on your side,
what gift will you bestow on me,
who agitated for revolt,
and freed you from that prison tower,
where you were held in misery?

SEGISMUNDO.

That tower itself shall be your prize.

There shall you languish 'til you die.
There is no call for traitors here,
now that the treachery is done.

BASILIO.
Your brilliance astounds us all.

ASTOLFO.
I never saw a man so changed.

ROSAURA.
So politic, so shrewd, so wise.

SEGISMUNDO.
Yet why should you be so amazed?
My teacher was a haunting dream,
my greatest fear, that I will wake
and find myself back in my chains.
Though it may never come to pass,
that dread will ever be with me.
And I have come to understand
that this too strange and happy state
is passing with a dreamlike speed.
Then let us love, and let's be glad,
enjoy what time is ours to have,
with honour may we always live,
quick to atone, quick to forgive.

The End.

Other Titles in this Series

Victoria Benedictsson
THE ENCHANTMENT
in a version by Clare Bayley

Anton Chekhov
THE CHERRY ORCHARD
trans. Stephen Mulrine
THE SEAGULL
trans. Stephen Mulrine
THREE SISTERS
in a version by Nicholas Wright
UNCLE VANYA
trans. Stephen Mulrine

Johann Wolfgang von Goethe
FAUST – PARTS ONE & TWO
in a version by Howard Brenton

Nikolai Gogol
THE GOVERNMENT
INSPECTOR
trans. Stephen Mulrine

Maxim Gorky
CHILDREN OF THE SUN
trans. Stephen Mulrine

Henrik Ibsen
A DOLL'S HOUSE
trans. Kenneth McLeish
AN ENEMY OF THE PEOPLE
in a version by Arthur Miller
GHOSTS
trans. Stephen Mulrine
HEDDA GABLER
in a version by Richard Eyre
JOHN GABRIEL BORKMAN
in a version by Nicholas Wright
THE LADY FROM THE SEA
trans. Kenneth McLeish
THE MASTER BUILDER
trans. Kenneth McLeish
PEER GYNT
trans. Kenneth McLeish
ROSMERSHOLM
in a version by Mike Poulton
THE WILD DUCK
trans. Stephen Mulrine